DARING LEADERS BOLD IDEAS

BOLD IDEAS

DARING LEADERS BOLD IDEAS DARING LEADERS

BOLD IDEAS

DARING LEADERS BOLD IDEAS

DARING LEADERS BOLD IDEAS DARING LEADERS

BOLD IDEAS DARING LEADERS BOLD IDEAS

DARING LEADERS BOLD IDEAS DARING LEADERS

BOLD IDEAS DARING LEADERS BOLD IDEAS

DARING LEADERS BOLD IDEAS DARING LEADERS

BOLD IDEAS DARING LEADERS BOLD IDEAS

DARING LEADERS BOLD IDEAS

DARING LEADERS BOLD IDEAS DARING LEADERS

BOLD IDEAS DARING LEADERS BOLD IDEAS

DARING LEADERS BOLD IDEAS DARING LEADERS

BOLD IDEAS DARING LEADERS BOLD IDEAS DARING LEADERS

BOLD IDEAS DARING LEADERS BOLD IDEAS

Dear Marshall,

You exemplify leadership, humility, and generosity. Your willingness to endorse this book truly lifted my courage to "ask" and I'm deeply honored to have your words on the back cover.

Thank you for all you've contributed to me + countless others through your transformative work.

With heartfelt gratitude,

Maria

1/2025

TWO FEET IN

Finding Clarity, Purpose, and Passion in Your Life and Career

Maria Cristini

ISBN: 979-8-9911685-0-2 (Paperback)

Library of Congress Control Number: 2024916739

Publisher • **Daring Leaders Bold Ideas**
www.DaringLeadersBoldIdeas.com

ORDERING INFORMATION
Quantity sales. Special discounts are available on quantity purchases by corporations, associations, and others. For details contact publisher.

Book Design and chapter illustrations • **Aleksandra Jelic**
Cover art and illustrations at the start of each chapter • **Dawood Marion**
Editor • **Isidra Mencos**
Copy Editor • **Jill Connaway**

I write this book with deep gratitude for the hundreds of clients who, over twenty years and thousands of coaching hours, have shared their boldest and most vulnerable dreams with me. Supporting the most impactful, innovative, bright, kind-spirited, and bold leaders I could ever know has inspired my unwavering love for humanity and great hope for our future.

I celebrate and deeply thank a lifetime of friends who have listened to my wild ideas, watched me slowly evolve into more of myself, and supported me, lifted me, or said nothing to deter me.

I share my admiration for my husband, Abrasha, who has always either backed my deepest dreams and highest visions or gotten out of my way, even when my desire made him uncomfortable. As I have grown and changed over the 30+ years we have been together, my life companion has loved me unconditionally. This has been a true gift.

I dedicate this book to my children, Dimitri and Ruben, so they can choose to read a few thoughts or look at a particular section, as they are so inclined. Nurturing and watching them develop into extraordinary, intentional, empathetic, determined, creative, and loving men has been my joy and honor.

If you're a young adult reading this book, I'm excited to share perspectives with you from which you can pick and choose to create your own framework for life. For the experienced leader, this book is my way of sharing, and possibly reminding you of what you already know, wisdom learned over the years.

My purpose always is to nurture and empower you to be the best version you can possibly imagine of yourself and to encourage you to ask yourself a few questions as you embark on the always-evolving future next step.

ACKNOWLEDGMENTS

I want to thank my teachers, mentors, and coaches who taught me my craft, and from whom I gathered my tools. I'm grateful to have had the opportunity to engage in hundreds of hours of workshops where coaching demonstrations inspired my desire to want to be masterful at what is the art and science of coaching.

Rich Fettke was the first coach whose workshop I attended to learn about coaching, after which I encouraged my husband to hire him—and he did.

Co-Active Training Institute (formerly The Coaches Training Institute) is where I started training in January 2000 and was fully certified as a Certified Professional Co-Active Coach (CPCC) in August 2001. Co-Active Training Institute is recognized as the most rigorous and respected coaching training and certification program in the industry. The CPCC designation is the global "gold standard" in coaching certification. I use what I learned there to this day. The first three chapters of this book, the foundation of all my coaching relationships, are inspired by the coaching tools I learned through my Co-Active training. The Wheel of Life in Chapter 1 is an adaptation of a copyrighted version from Co-Active Training Institute.

During my second Co-Active workshop, I watched a coaching demonstration led by Mai Vu and Phillip Sandahl, and in that moment a voice within me excitedly stated, "If I could do that, I would be so happy." I am. Thank you to Mai and Phil for your vibrancy and passion while teaching and coaching.

Leza Danly, the founder of Lucid Living, was my first coach. Her own inspirations, work, and materials have had a tremendous impact on my perspective, life, and coaching work. I learned the concept of a Joyous Adult and Joyous Responsibility from her, and I am forever grateful, as this work has transformed me and, in turn, the lives of so many of my clients. Her work is now an integral part of me, and the learnings I've integrated are sprinkled throughout this book, particularly in Chapter 12. I want to honor her, our conversations, and my time participating in Lucid Living workshops.

Before all of that happened, my cousin, Anna DiMascio, who has known me my entire life, wrote in an email, "I know someone who is studying to be a life coach...you may want to look into this, you do it all the time anyway." She introduced me to the idea of becoming a professional coach, something I knew nothing about. After that, Allison Feeley, my girlfriend since eighth grade and a therapist who I thought might scoff at the idea of coaching, instead encouraged me every step of the way, along with taking some of the same courses I loved so much to integrate into her own work. And I'm forever grateful to Steven LaFrance for introducing me to the social sector, and for generously referring me to his network of visionary leaders time and again.

In moving this book from the idea phase to something to share with others, I want to thank people who championed me: Celia Tejada, my dear friend whose passion and vision inspires me; Sally Grisedale, my coaching colleague who told me to "throw it over the fence" to my writing coach and editor Isidra Mencos when I was stuck; and Dawood Marion, whose stories inspired my writing.

I want to acknowledge my parents, for it's in the struggle to become ourselves that we find our own strength, courage, and determination. As most, I did struggle to be myself in my childhood home environment, while surrounded by love. The noes I received have become my clients' "YES you can"!

IT TAKES A VILLAGE!

Dear Reader,

Coaching has changed my life. Both the coaching I have received and the coaching I have given others have transformed me. In supporting my clients, I have gained much learning, inspiration, and the opportunity to give the best of myself through our conversations.

Since I may not get to have an actual conversation with you, I'm compelled to write the very thoughts that I've repeatedly explored over the last two decades. *Two Feet In* allows me to offer you the same approach I've been using with my clients to help you achieve your highest and boldest dreams and aspirations.

This book is divided into two distinct parts:

Part One (Chapters 1–3) is very interactive. You will fill in the **Wheel of Life** to make note of where you are now in all the important areas of your life. Then you will reflect on where you want to be for each of those areas—your ideal vision.

This exercise will offer you perspective and a holistic view. It will help you see **the gap between where you are now and where you want to be**. You will better understand where there is room for creating change and where there will be growth that comes with meeting your personal challenges. You will also be more keenly aware of opportunities you can take advantage of or create. This gap reflects the beautiful journey to manifesting your visions.

I will then ask you to reflect on your **core values**, because when you achieve goals that honor your core values, you will feel fulfilled and joyous.

Once you have defined your core values, you will start work on **closing the gap**. You will focus on one to three areas where you want to see significant change in the short-term and set **six-month goals with measurable results**.

This structured approach, which you can repeat every six months, will define your dreams and help you achieve them step-by-step.

When people set goals, they are typically linear. They think, "Okay, I'm going to do *x, y,* and *z,* and then I'm going to achieve my goal." But it rarely works that smoothly. You are bound to run into setbacks, encounter all types of distractions, bump up against your own lingering resistance, and be faced with fear of the chaos associated with change or even fear of success as your imagination runs wild with all the possible scenarios swirling in your mind.

Part Two (Chapters 4–12) provides **a framework for your evolution**, as well as **inspiration** and **support** for whenever you get stuck. I encourage you to read these chapters through once, so you can anticipate the issues you may encounter and be better prepared to address them. Then, as you run into a challenge in the pursuit of your goals, you can go back to the chapter that discusses that particular issue and find guidance and coaching moments to navigate it.

For example, if you feel unsupported, you will benefit from re-reading chapter 4 (You're Never Alone) to remind yourself of strategies for tapping into your network. Or, if you feel your commitment wavering, you can get a boost by re-reading chapter 5 (Two Feet In) to gather more strength and clarity about what you need to do to keep moving forward.

It may also be fun to simply open the book to a random page and use it as a reminder or message for your day.

The combination of Chapters 1–3 with Chapters 4–12 will give you the closest replica to what my clients experience in our coaching relationship. The first three chapters are equivalent to the first three intake calls I do with my clients. After that, we have regularly scheduled calls, where the topics in Chapters 4–12 come up in no particular order. The same challenges that prompt me to share these thoughts with my clients are bound to come up for you. When they do, you will be able to pick up this book, and find the support that has helped my clients achieve their personal and professional goals. I've shared these perspectives over and over with them with excellent results.

A LIFE WELL LIVED FOCUSES ON JOY, as does this book. By using Part One to set a clear framework for your life, and Part Two as a source of inspiration and support, I hope to facilitate your journey towards living a successful, fulfilling, and joyous life.

Warmly,

P.S. Be sure to visit page 121 for exclusive resources and gifts just for you!

PART

ONE

1

GAINING PERSPECTIVE

Start Right Where You Are

When you want to create change in your life by launching something new or taking what exists to the next level, it's important to start by taking inventory of exactly how things are now. By knowing where you are and where you want to go, the gap reveals itself. This information gives you the overview from which you can create a strategy to get to where you want to be.

For that purpose, I'm particularly fond of the Wheel of Life exercise, because it gives a holistic view of your full life. Keep in mind that although it provides twelve distinct areas to reflect on, they are all intertwined and impact each other.

 ## Where Are You Now?

Grab a notebook or start a new document on your computer for these coaching exercises. Think about your current life circumstances, and jot down some notes to reflect what you're feeling and what the circumstances are like now in each of these twelve areas of your life. A few lines will suffice. For example:

Home: *I live in a rental apartment in downtown Portland. It's small and it doesn't have a balcony, but it's cozy. I share the apartment with a roommate.*

LIFE AREAS:

Home
Office Space (in and/or out of the home)
Career
Finances
Health & Fitness
Friends & Community
Family

Significant Other
Personal Development
Spirituality
Fun & Recreation
Other (name your own area):
Contribution, Creativity, Public Speaking, Parenting, Confidence, Leadership, Professional Impact, Legacy, etc.

Now, think about how fulfilled and satisfied you are in each of these areas of your life, and on a scale of 1–10, with 1 = lowest satisfaction to 10 = highest satisfaction, rate each area in your notebook or document.

Once you have your ratings for each of the twelve areas, you can color the individual sections of the Wheel of Life to the level of satisfaction you selected. For example, if you rated your Home area an 8, you will color in the first eight sections of that area.

Here is an example of a filled-in Wheel of Life, where the "Other" area is Professional Impact.

Now fill in your own Wheel of Life, choosing your own category for the "Other" section, which is the blank section in the following illustration.

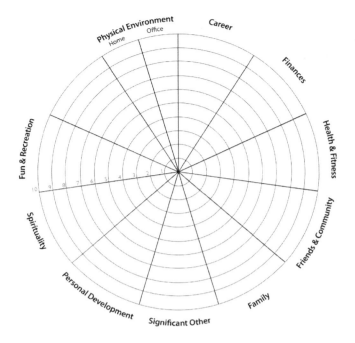

How fulfilled and satisfied are you?

When you finish rating and coloring in your Wheel of Life, your new, uneven circumference will likely show you where you feel the ups and downs of life, the areas that bring you the most joy and those that drain you. You'll have a visual of where your life feels in or out of balance. The areas you rated 8, 9, and 10 are most likely where your natural talents, character, and learned skills and values (which we'll discuss in Chapter 2) are currently engaged and honored, and you feel joy.

In the areas that you rated lower than an 8, you may be feeling something between malaise and unhappiness. Take heart: what helped you create success in the areas with higher numbers can be applied to the other areas of your life. For example, if you feel joy in your life area of Friends & Community but gave a low rating to Career, pause and assess what makes you a good friend, what keeps you connected, and how you are open and willing to try new things in this area where you are comfortable. Next, you can consider how you might transfer and apply those skills and talents to the area of Career. As a starting point, how can you bring the same qualities that helped you create a joyful life with friends and community into your Career?

COACHING MOMENT

It's not realistic or the intended goal to have 10s in all areas all the time. Of course, there will be some days when life feels like all 10s, and that's great fun, but it's not likely to stay at that euphoric level; life always brings up challenges or a desire to grow further. What filling in the Wheel of Life will inspire is a smoother journey with ups and downs in the upper numbers. The graphic will show you where you can apply yourself to feel more joyous and fulfilled. By noting where your experiences are most positive, you can remember your foundation of strength, so that when you have a big dip in one area, you can regain your mojo more quickly in that aspect of your life by applying what you do well naturally.

This exercise also points out that there are many areas in life, and to feel fulfilled, they each need their own vision and dedication of time. Sometimes people get so wrapped up with one area that they dismiss the other aspects exist. In the midst of hard deadlines, my clients often dismiss the value of Fun & Recreation. Their Career and Finances may be booming, but their meaningful experiences with Friends and Family go out the window. The Wheel of Life makes evident the lack of balance and the gaps between where you are and where you want to be. That awareness is the first step towards achieving a less bumpy ride.

What Do You Know of Your Dreams?

If you could wave a magic wand and create your ideal life, what would your joyous future look and feel like in terms of Physical Environment (Home and Office), Career, Finances, Health & Fitness, Friends & Community, Family, Significant Other, Personal Development, Spirituality, Fun & Recreation, or other area(s) you care about? What would make each of these areas of your life a 10 out of 10 as far as fulfillment, satisfaction, and joy? In other words: What are your dreams?

Dreams are always evolving but in this very moment you have longings, an inkling, an idea, or complete clarity about what yours are.

Take the opportunity to really think of your life in terms of big picture vision, without worrying yet about goals or timelines. This is a moment for free visioning to define your aspirations. Think of the end of your life, or, if that's too far out, think twenty years from now. What will your joyous life be like?

Where Do You Want to Be?

Take some time to write what YOU want in each area of your life in your notebook or document. For example:

Home: *My home is modern, with an open floor plan and wooden floors. It's filled with light, with large windows, and a beautiful view. I love that the location is within walking distance to coffee shops, restaurants, and a bookstore, which creates a sense of community.*

This home could be a city home with a view of downtown or the ocean, or a country home with views of gardens and hillsides or a lake. Be as specific as possible while remaining open to possibilities of something even better.

COACHING MOMENT

This life vision is about what you desire, not what you think this area of your life "should" look like or what others in your life want for you. Review what you wrote and make sure you did not write anyone else's dream for your life; if so, go back and write what's authentic to your own vision at this time.

Now look at your dreams/future visions as you wrote them and ask yourself about:

YOUR DREAMS' SCOPE AND AUTHENTICITY

- Is this dream big enough? "Enough" is a key word here: big and daring enough yet rightsized.
- Am I playing small and/or holding back due to fear, lack of confidence, or lack of vision and clarity?
- Do these dreams authentically reflect my desires?

YOUR FEELINGS AND COMMITMENT

- Do I really care to create the outcome I'm writing about?
- Does it excite me to look forward to this life?
- Will I feel proud of my life as I envision it?
- Do I feel passionate about engaging in the effort to make these dreams a reality?
- Am I happy to be responsible for these dreams?

THE CONNECTION BETWEEN YOUR DREAMS AND YOUR COMMUNITY

- Does this dream contribute to the life vision I have for myself and the world I care about living in?
- What am I receiving in pursuit of this dream?
- What am I contributing?

Edit what you wrote until your big picture/life dreams truly represent YOUR desires, as you know them now. Be specific and vivid with the essence of your vision. Write life dreams that are big enough and heartfelt, so that when they are realized, you will feel YOURS is a life well-lived in every area.

When I type my clients' visions, I write them as if the person is stating the facts in the future. I encourage you to place yourself in your optimal future and write your ideal future visions (10 out of 10 as far as fulfillment, satisfaction, and joy) as if you were there, living them.

Feel free to update your future vision(s) any time as you become more intimate with your own dreams and desires.

COACHING MOMENT

We can only live in the present, but having a future focus guides our next action steps, our choice making, our demeanor, and our outlook. Having a future vision increases our ability to see opportunities when they cross our path; it guides us to know what to look for and inspires us to create, which increases our courage.

Notice the Gap

The difference between where you are now and where you want to be in each life area is the gap. In some areas, you'll feel very proud and joy-filled, as the gap is minimal or non-existent. In other areas, you'll recognize there's work to be done, and the work feels doable. Yet, in other life areas, the gap may appear enormous.

Keep in mind that by focusing on the areas that are easier to improve first, often the others lift naturally in response or become easier to lift later. With this approach you will gain confidence and momentum. Soon the big gaps will not be as difficult to improve upon as you might imagine.

Later in this process, you will choose and set focus areas for your near-term goals, but, for now, simply reflect on all the work you've done in answering these questions. Acknowledge where you are now and the beautiful dreams of the future that you hold. Let it in. Awareness is key, because it's the pivot point of change. You are already much further ahead than most!

Reimagine Your Team

You may have heard the adage, "Show me who your friends are, and I'll tell you who you are." I don't quite agree with this sentiment. I believe you can have many friends and acquaintances, for many reasons, and from various parts of your life, but they are not all a reflection of who you are today.

What is truly important is who are the people you spend the most time with on a regular basis. According to research by social psychologist Dr. David McClelland of Harvard, your reference group [people you habitually associate with] determines as much as 95 percent of your success or failure in life.

It's worth asking yourself: Who do you talk with daily and weekly? Do the people in your closest circle **LIFT**, **INSPIRE**, and **SUPPORT** you? Are they nurturing your vision, your dreams, and your accomplishments as you nurture theirs? When you first give birth to a new dream, idea, vision, or goal, do you have one, two, or three people to share it with that will remain open, listen deeply, and ask questions for clarity without shutting down your thoughts and stifling your desire to fly?

People who support you in dreaming and gaining clarity will ask open-ended questions to help you move forward such as, "What's your motivation? How do you envision the process to make your dream a reality? What might it look like if it becomes real?"

You want to share your fledgling idea only with specific people who will naturally encourage you to think deeper and infuse you with inspiration and courage. And when it comes to the "how"—how to move your vision forward—this mini team becomes resourceful, supportive, and solutions oriented.

Your Core Team

List here or in your notebook/document the people whom you associate with on a daily and weekly basis, outside of your immediate family. If there are a few more (or less) than five, it's okay:

1

2

3

4

5

Think about this short list for a moment. Do these people in your closest circle **LIFT**, **INSPIRE**, and **SUPPORT** you?

The people whom you are in touch with most often make up your core team. They have the power to support **who you are becoming**. It's crucial to choose them well.

As you grow and evolve, you may need to shift at least some of the people in this group from people who supported your past self to people who support your future vision. This doesn't mean that you stop speaking to friends who no longer align with who you're becoming and what you are creating. Yet, you may find that you talk with them less often, as people who align with your dreams (and current six-month goals) become part of your inner circle.

For example, when I was raising my children, I had five friends who were very close. We raised our children together, saw each other all the time, and the kids were like cousins. Now, we still stay in touch, but I see them maybe five times a year. As projects, circumstances, and dreams change, so do some core team members.

COACHING MOMENT

When you have a new dream, you want to choose carefully the one to three people who you share it with. Choose only the few who will seek to understand your vision and support you in figuring it out, with or without their direct input. Choose people who trust your ability to be discerning and care more about how your idea impacts you and others vs. how it may impact them. If you do this, your tiny seed of an idea has a chance to grow. Otherwise, it may be squashed on day one.

Your Extended Network

Make a list of all your friends and loved ones. Include your childhood friends, relatives that you enjoy being with, people with whom you like to dance, hike, dine, engage in a sport, or go to the theater, ballet, or ballgame. Add people you travel with; include friends you lived with in college or people you are raising your kids with. Add fun colleagues, people who were very close to you during past projects, and people from various groups, activities, or communities you participate in that you also meet for lunch, coffee, or a gathering after work.

This might be a very long list. Let's keep it to people you have a relationship with other than via social media.

These friends are not "who you are." They are reflections of the various phases in your life, the many parts of you, and your varied interests—a lifetime of friends. Honor them by taking inventory and remembering the love and energy you gain from each one specifically.

Although most of these friends are not part of your core team right now, they form your extended network. The ones you are closest with are often the people who, when you connect, you immediately feel comfortable with and are able to pick up right where you left off.

There's comfort in being with longtime companions who know you. You can go back to them for advice, for a connection to other people they know, or to compare notes about a certain topic you're both interested in. Also, if you realize that your core team of five or so people is not really lifting you and inspiring you to live your best life, looking at this longer list may remind you of someone whom you have lost touch with but could be an ideal person to reconnect with and possibly bring into your inner circle.

1. ....
2. ....
3. ....
4. ....
5. ....
6. ....
7. ....
8. ....
9. ....
10. ....
11. ....
12. ....
13. ....
14. ....
15. ....
16. ....
17. ....
18. ....
19. ....
20. ....
21. ....
22. ....
23. ....
24. ....
25. ....

26. ....
27. ....
28. ....
29. ....
30. ....
31. ....
32. ....
33. ....
34. ....
35. ....
36. ....
37. ....
38. ....
39. ....
40. ....
41. ....
42. ....
43. ....
44. ....
45. ....
46. ....
47. ....
48. ....
49. ....
50. ....

51

52

53

54

55

56

57

58

59

60

61

62

63

64

65

66

67

68

69

70

71

72

73

74

75

76

77

78

79

80

81

82

83

84

85

86

87

88

89

90

91

92

93

94

95

96

97

98

99

100

CORE VALUES:
Your Roadmap to Joy

Your Guidance System

You now have an overview and a personal assessment of your life in every area. You know your dreams for the future and which close friends and colleagues will lift, inspire, and support you in who you want to become and what you want to create. It's time to turn to the foundational work of discovering and claiming your core values.

YOUR CORE VALUES ARE YOUR PERSONAL ROADMAP TO A JOYOUS ADULTHOOD, FULFILLMENT, FEELING IN FLOW, SERENDIPITY, OPPORTUNITY, AND LIVING LIFE IN ALIGNMENT WITH YOUR TRUTH AND YOUR SPIRIT.

By doing this work before you set goals to close the gap, you are "slowing down now to speed up later."

A value is core if you feel joy when it's honored, whether it is happening to you, or to another person or people. For example, if one of your core values is "self-expression," you will feel joyous when you're expressing yourself freely, such as sharing your opinions in a work meeting with confidence. You'll also feel joy when you experience a child on a school stage or an adult across the world able to authentically express themselves through their words, actions, and/or emotions.

Likewise, you know when a value is core if you feel angry or frustrated when yours is not being honored.

As an example, I have a core value connected to "evolving." If I put myself in situations where I am stimulated by new concepts that help me grow and evolve, this core value is honored, and I feel joy. But if I am in a situation where my growth is stifled and I don't have choices or access to what I want and need to grow, I'm going to feel angry, closed in, and frustrated.

Others can also say or do things that crush your core values. If "harmony" is your core value and you witness your supervisor inappropriately yelling at a co-worker, you may find yourself feeling anxious and upset, because your core values of love, respect, and harmony are being crushed. In that moment, you can decide, "Am I going to let it slide, or do I want to say something?"

COACHING MOMENT

Core values don't change over time. Depending at what age you create your list of values, the words used to express them may change but not the essence. How you manifest and honor them will change. There are endless ways you can honor your values. Perhaps today you express yourself by being vocal in work meetings, and in a few years, you will self-express by writing and publishing essays or a book. You may have a core value of helping, fairness, and equity; as a young person, you may have been the one that stood by the underdog in school, and as an adult, you become a criminal defense lawyer. As a young person, not knowing better, the values of power, presence, and leadership may have compelled you to be a bully and egotistically competitive, and as an adult, you find yourself being an athletic coach bringing out the best in each team member. Someone who values beauty and self-care may be a model in their youth, and later, decide to run a nonprofit getting stunning wigs onto the heads of people who have lost their hair to cancer or another illness.

Once you know your core values, it's fun to think about how they manifested over the years from a young teen to the present and how they may manifest in the future.

Your Values Word Bank

In this exercise, you are going to, first, create a word bank of as many of your values that come to mind; then, you will do another pass to define your core values. You will most likely find that your secondary values are directly related to your core values.

1 Re-read all that you wrote about your Life Areas ideal vision, and this time, highlight any value words. Value words reflect the intangibles that bring joy such as freedom, love, justice, connection, intimacy, etc. (Intangible means that you cannot touch them, i.e., is not an object.) For example, in the description of your ideal home you may highlight three to five words that point to your intangible core values: *My home is **modern**, with an **open** floor plan, and wooden floors. It's filled with **light**, with large windows, and a **beautiful** view. I love that the location is within walking distance to coffee shops, restaurants, and a bookstore, which creates a sense of **community**.*

2 Look at your list of close friends, and write what you admire about them, such as: creativity, humor, loyalty, honesty, optimism, etc.

3 Look at your life and make note of the values expressed in the following:

PHYSICAL ENVIRONMENT: Do you collect art, books, culinary equipment, bikes, cameras, tech gadgets, sports equipment, tools? What values are reflected in your linens, living room décor, and even the car you drive? What values are reflected in the elements that make your physical environment unique?

FINANCES: Look at your records (payments made and received, credit/debit statements, savings) and notice: What are you spending money on? Who are you receiving money from and for what? What are you saving for, or are you not saving? What values are reflected through your home mortgage or rent, investments, education expenses, restaurant and grocery spending, your charitable contributions, fun and recreation expenses, clothing expenditures, pets care, expenses for your children and/or loved ones? What values are reflected and being honored through your spending?

PEOPLE: Think about the people in your life, especially the people you most enjoy spending time with. Why is that? What values are honored when you spend time together?

WHAT PISSES YOU OFF: During the next few days, notice what aggravates and enrages you. Is it the driver in front of you? The slow service at a store or a restaurant? The parent raging on a child as you pass them on the street? The adult that just dropped their empty coffee cup on the ground? The neighbors cutting or not cutting their tree? Hidden in the aggravations are values being crushed by you or another, such as wisdom, intelligence, efficiency, respect, harmony, love, beauty, etc. Make note of the values that are being crushed.

WHAT BRINGS YOU JOY: Again, over the next few days, notice what brings you a sense of happiness, laughter, pride. What pleases you? In those joys and pleasures your values are being honored. Make sure you jot down what the values are.

WHAT ACTIVITIES DO YOU LOVE MOST: Do you love the theater, being in nature, traveling the world, painting, playing music, scuba diving, hang gliding? Those activities are special to you because they honor your values. What values are being honored when you are engaged in them? As an example: traveling may be honoring the values of learning, exposure, adventure, freedom, etc. Going to a theater performance may be honoring the values of self-expression, perspective, or mastery. Whatever values your favorite activities honor, add them to your growing list.

As you take a few days to allow your values to reveal themselves to you, building a robust list of most or **all your values**, you will end up with **your values word bank.**

Your Core Values, Defined

It's now time to embrace the second phase of this exercise: finding your core values among all those beautiful words.

I like to create this list by forming strings of three value words that are related to each other. I like to use three words for each core value, because a value may mean different things to different people. For example, for me "freedom" may mean empowered and self-expressed, which means I'm joyous when I feel free, empowered, and self-expressed, but I also want that for all. For Michael, who is a serial entrepreneur, "freedom" may mean flexibility and choice. For Sara, who loves to be in nature and travel, "freedom" may mean adventure and exploration.

This is how a string will look:

Main Value Word | Descriptive Value Word | Descriptive Value Word

The two descriptive values are meant to express clearly what the core value means for YOU.

Here is my core values list. I provide it only as an example. Only you truly know what your core values are and how you enjoy honoring them, so your list will look quite different than mine.

At the core, I value ...

Intimacy | Connection | Unconditional Love

Freedom | Empowerment | Self-Expression

Learning | Growth | Evolving

Magic | Metaphysical | Divine

Impact | Transformation | Serendipity

Passion | Clarity | Purpose

Aesthetics | Beauty | Creativity (in nature and manmade)

Ease | Elegance | Trust (the Universe has your back)

Childlike-Innocence | Carefree | Fun

Harmony | Peace | Synergy

Optimism | Idealism | Hope

You can see that some of my values, if not all of them, are being honored in the creation of this book and in you reading it.

Your Core Values List

Now it's your turn. This phase of the exercise has two parts:

1 Take the word bank you just created, and:

- Make groupings (word strings) of values you feel are related, as you see fit. Example: Opportunity | Freedom | Exploration

- Now put the main value word, the word that captures the most meaning for you, at the front of the row. Example: Freedom | Opportunity | Exploration

2 Create value strings. Aim for a list of between 8–12 rows, each line consisting of three words. That said, the list doesn't have to be perfect. You may find that in one row you have four values but aiming for three will create a more succinct list that will resonate quickly with you when you look at it. The clearer and more succinct you can make your list, the more benefit it will provide you over time.

Creating your personal values list will offer you many benefits:

- Simply reading your list will re-connect you to your own core.

- If you're having a bad day, and you take a moment to consciously honor any of your core values, you'll lift your own energy immediately.

- You can use it as a decision-making tool by comparing the choices you're faced with to your core values to see how many would get honored by each possible choice. When you're truly joyous, multiple values are being honored simultaneously.

- If you're upset or angry and aren't clear why, look at your list to see what values are being crushed, and you'll get closer to knowing what to do or say.

COACHING MOMENT

There is nothing wrong with feeling the emotion of anger. It's what we do with it that can be a problem. Anger lets us know that a boundary has been crossed. Either someone has done something that crosses our boundaries and/or crushes our values, and we then feel angry, or we have done that to ourselves. We can cross our own boundaries by giving too much of ourselves or by being too nice when not warranted; and when we don't honor our own core values we will feel our anger rise.

The ideal is to be aware of your anger and pause a moment to get curious about what is going on. Why are you feeling upset and/or resentful? That moment of reflection and awareness can be enough to get you back to honoring your core values or help you figure out an appropriate response when someone else is involved.

Through your attention to this list, your life will become a reflection of your values, where each day, what you do, who you're with, and where you put your love, focus, and attention brings you joy.

3

FINDING YOUR

Behind Every No There's a Yes

Now that you've laid the groundwork to create your dream life aligned with your core values, you need to say YES to each step in the pursuit of your goals.

The word yes, when said from the heart, initiates an opening, agreement, and permission— permission you grant yourself—to go after your dreams.

This doesn't mean that you're saying yes to everything. What it means is that when you say no to something or someone, you are saying yes to something else that is more important to you at this time. I often ask my clients, **"What's the yes behind your no?"** For example, if someone asks you to volunteer on a committee, and you don't have time for that because you're busy with a personal project, you will say no to the committee, because you're saying yes to your own project.

It's a good idea to share your yes with others, because it creates intimacy vs. the separation a no can create. In the example above, instead of saying, "No, I can't be on the committee," you may say, "I'm sorry, I can't participate on your committee right now, because I'm fully focused on designing a course for young people, and that's taking a lot of my time." What you are saying yes to is designing the course; that's your guidepost. In sharing that with the person who wanted to recruit you for the committee, instead of just saying no, you're helping them know you better. They may even get curious about your project and become a helpful resource.

Whether saying yes to yourself or another, slow down enough to find your yes and live life from that place.

Ignite Your Future: Clearing the Path to Your YES Life

What's standing between you and living your YES life?

Even when you know what your dreams are, you may find yourself resisting the steps that will take you there. **Sometimes, you don't grant yourself permission to pursue your highest vision. Other times, you lack clarity about your goals or the specific outcomes you're after, and you misinterpret it as being lazy.** You may also worry about a negative outcome or failure. You might hold back from a great project when you're feeling constricted and being driven by your own fears or sense of powerlessness. Perhaps you're not truly aligned, and what you say you want is not what you really want.

There's an internal process to get from a knee-jerk no to a definitive YES, and that process involves clear vision, passion for what you're agreeing to, and imagination for a positive outcome.

Permission

Are you holding back on giving yourself full permission to go for your dreams?

Perhaps you have an idea for a book, but you feel scared to write it. You may come up with a list of why nots, such as: I haven't earned a PhD in the topic. I'm not a writer. What I have to say can't possibly matter. Others have already addressed this topic. I don't have enough authority.

Yet, if you have a good idea to share, say YES to your vision. You can always do more research, get feedback, and hire an editor to polish your writing.

THE FIRST STEP TO ACHIEVING ANY GOAL IS GIVING YOURSELF PERMISSION TO DEVOTE TIME AND ATTENTION TO YOUR DESIRE.

Remember that you're the adult in charge of your life. The only parental guidance, rules, restrictions, and freedoms you experience come from you. If you want something, and it's aligned with your core values (and within the law of course), go for it!

Feeling Lazy?

You've decided to write the book, but it's not happening. You may wonder, "Why am I not getting it done?" You start beating yourself up. You feel inefficient, frustrated, unmotivated, and maybe even useless, or maybe you're simply not thrilled by what you're engaged with. You're probably thinking, **"Am I lazy?"**

No! You are NOT LAZY!
When people start wondering about their laziness—I'm lazy. Maybe I'm lazy. I'm being lazy. Or, I know I'm not lazy, but ...—what's typically happening is that there is a lack of clarity and vision, and subsequently, a lack of internal drive.

If you are not clear, and you don't have a vision for the next stage of your life (the upcoming week, month, year, decade), your next steps will be obscured, so of course, you will not know what to do. You will do close to nothing or simply what comes your way to fill the void, and you'll equate that sense of lethargy to being lazy.

Following the book example, perhaps you don't have full clarity on what the structure of the book should be or where to start. You're not lazy ... you're unclear, and instead of doing something stupid or wasting time and resources heading in the wrong direction, you're choosing to stay safe by doing very little.

The next time you're feeling lazy, look to your own sense of clarity, vision, and internal drive and direction; if those are all missing, acknowledge it. You will then be halfway towards taking meaningful action.

COACHING MOMENT

Ask yourself:
- Based on what I know now, what would I like to be doing?
- If I did that, would I feel happy that I tried it one month and/or one year from now?
- If that's true, what's the tiniest first step in the direction of that goal/dream?

What drives you is your WHY, your motivation. When you are connected to your WHY, you will feel expansive and driven. Here are some examples of what you might be feeling when you're expansive and driven versus constricted and stalled.

EXPANSIVE	POWERFUL	CONSTRICTED	POWERLESS
Loving	Hateful
Passionate	Apathetic
Courageous	Fearful
Generous	Greedy
Connected	Derailed
Clear	Confused
Open	Withholding

Think about the times when nothing was going to stop you. You were on fire, and a successful outcome was the only option. You knew what was driving you, your WHY, and you were fully expanded and going for it. You didn't even know how you would make something happen, but you were all in and willing. I hope you've experienced this state a number of times in your life, so that you can draw upon it, and remember your capacity, energy, and endless drive.

COACHING MOMENT

If you were to think of six words to describe how you are feeling and being when in that expansive state and six words to represent how you feel and act when in your constricted state, what would your words be?

EXPANSIVE	CONSTRICTED

OUR MOST MEMORABLE PROJECTS, ENGAGEMENTS, AND DECISIONS ARE DRIVEN BY PASSION FOR AN OUTCOME, LOVE OF PEOPLE, AND/OR BEING OF SERVICE IN SOME WAY.

In times when these motivations drive us, we dig deep into the fullness of all we know, use the sum of our experiences, and are unafraid of the unknown. If you want to live and work fearlessly, and feel driven and determined, start by answering the following questions:

- What's the boldest thing you could dedicate yourself to out of love, passion, and/or service?

- What would have you wake up energized?

- What would bring you joy to see manifested?

"If not now, then when?"

— Hillel

COACHING MOMENT

Do you allow yourself to connect to your own passion? Are you feeling connected to whom and what you love, to those you want to be of service to, or to the project you would like to see completed, if for no one else's sake but your own? Are you giving yourself permission to live the life you will be proud of as you take your last breath?

What do you want to accomplish, enjoy, and see to have a life of no regrets?

- Even if you never accomplish everything on your list, why not try?

- What else are you doing with your time? Are you happy?

- Whatever your WHY, your motivation, your YES is, I encourage you to own it and let it drive you.

Alignment ... or the Lack of it

You need alignment between what you say you want, what you truly want, and what you can handle. Sometimes people set a dream that's too big or too far out into the future. For example, a new coach may say, "I want ten new clients in the next month." That's a huge undertaking! Of course, any coach would want ten new clients, but to get them in only one month is an enormous goal; not knowing how to create that outcome or how to manage it if it manifested might result in paralysis. Instead, if the stated goal was, "I want three new clients in the next two months," there would be more alignment between the goal and what is actually manageable, and it's much more likely that the coach will achieve their goal.

Also, if what you say you want is not aligned with your core values, you may sabotage yourself unconsciously. For example, if you want to make $100K a year, but you are looking for jobs that are not aligned with your core values, it will slow you down. Perhaps you won't put full effort into tailoring your CV and cover letters, and as a result, you won't get the interview.

WHEN OUR SHORT-TERM GOALS ARE NOT ALIGNED WITH OUR BIG PICTURE VISION AND VALUES, WE HOLD OURSELVES BACK.

When there is alignment, we get excited, and we go full steam ahead; we figure out the steps, we use our network, and we do everything possible to reach our goals.

Your Primary Focus

You now know:
- Your future vision for your various life areas
- Your core values
- What drives, motivates, and expands you.

With that foundation, you are now ready to:
- Define your areas of Primary Focus and set realistic and meaningful short-term goals.
- Know your WHY, your motivation (goal setting with a twist).
- List your Measurable Results for each Primary Focus area.

You are now aware, from the Wheel of Life exercises, that Life Areas are intertwined and impact each other. As you work on a few goals in specific areas, many of your other Life Areas will improve as a result. If you work on Health & Fitness goals, your Career may improve as you gain energy, strength, and self-esteem. If you create a goal in Fun & Recreation, the Friends & Community and Family parts of your life may get a joyous boost.

With this in mind, I suggest you **choose three Primary Focus areas to work on over the next six months**.

COACHING MOMENT

Be sure your Primary Focus and measurable results are aligned with the Life Areas where you care to create change in the near future and with your core values. You want to spend your precious time and energy working on goals that will bring you joy.

Being responsible is joyous when you align the responsibility with your vision and values. For example, going to the dentist every six months may not be what you think of as joyous, but if it's connected to your vision of living a healthy life and to your value of self-care, health, or beauty, you can take pride in showing up for your dentist appointments on time.

Consider:

- If you choose three areas to give your serious focus to over the next six months, what would they be? What do you want to create or make happen? Where is it that you would like to see something change in the near future? If you are a young adult just starting your new career in an entry-level position, perhaps focusing on buying your dream home in the next six months is not realistic. It might make more sense to focus on the smaller steps such as growing your savings, learning how to increase your credit score, getting pre-approved for a mortgage, and making sure you're doing a great job in your new role, so you can improve your career and chances of long-term success; that will bring you closer to buying your dream home in the future.

- Why are you doing this? What are you really saying YES to? What's your motivation? This question requires a very honest answer, and sometimes it's tricky. You need to set aside ego motivations, as well as adolescent and childlike motivations. Ground yourself in your adult who truly wants what you are writing down and can be joyously responsible for creating it. For example, if one of your Primary Focus areas involves Fun & Recreation, and you decide in the next six months you will buy a convertible sports car, this is the time to think about it logistically: "This is the amount of money I have. This is the purpose for my car. These are my needs." Then you may opt for a car that is reasonable for you right now and won't break the bank, like a slightly used car and a brand that doesn't need a lot of expensive maintenance. If you let the adolescent take over, you might buy a car that looks cool, but you can hardly afford the monthly payments and maintenance, and it's overall less practical. If you let that happen, suddenly the convertible will quickly become a burden versus adding to your joyous Fun & Recreation.

- What are some measurable results that will indicate you have succeeded in meeting your six-month goals? You can choose progress steps and measures for every month or two as benchmarks. Ultimately, you want to know what key results will become evidence of your success. How will you know if you nailed your goal? In the case of the car, these measurable steps may be: Saving for the down payment, shopping for the car, test driving multiple cars, talking to a few dealers, improving your negotiating skills, researching insurance, and buying the car.

COACHING MOMENT

Think about the gap between where you are and where you want to be. What are the resources that will help you build a bridge to your future? List them all. You can have a coach, a mentor, and/or a key advocate or support team, specific goals, measurable results, action steps, and strategies.

 ### Three Primary Focus areas for Six-Month Goals

Fill out the following information in your notebook/document three times. (It's like granting yourself three wishes.) You are, in effect, making a clear promise to yourself.

PRIMARY FOCUS: WHAT'S THE OVERARCHING GOAL YOU WANT TO MANIFEST IN THE NEXT SIX-MONTHS?
What's the overarching goal in this area? What do you want to be true?

WHY: What's your motivation? Why do you want this to be true?

MEASURABLE RESULTS:
What will be true when this area/goal has manifested? What will be the evidence that it happened? How will you know you've succeeded?

If your Primary Focus involves a big overall goal that may take longer than six months to complete, make note of benchmark results for six months from now.

Next are examples of how to think of goals and how I write them with my clients.

FOCUS AREA: TO GET COMFORTABLE AT PUBLIC SPEAKING

WHY:

• To step into my own leadership.

• To learn how to move a room of people into action.

• To start preparing for a long-term goal of making a living as a public speaker.

MEASURABLE RESULTS:

• Enroll in a local Toastmaster group and attend weekly.

• Schedule to speak at my company's all-hands meeting in six months.

• In month one, prepare a short presentation for Toastmasters and refine it.

• In months two and three, prepare a draft of my work presentation and show it to trusted colleagues to get feedback.

• In month four, refine the presentation.

• In month five, rehearse and prepare to present it at the all-hands meeting in month six.

• In month six, give an engaging presentation at my company's all-hands meeting.

Other goals might sound like this (and you would write them up as Primary Focus/Why/ Measurable Results, as above):

If your focus area is Health & Fitness, your overarching goal may be to get your body toned and strong, gain a certain amount of muscle mass, or increase endurance for aerobic exercise. The WHY is to have more energy. Your measurable steps can include enrolling in a gym and going three times a week, taking up daily running and adding more minutes every four weeks, or starting to bike to work.

If you added Confidence in the Other category of your Life Areas, and that is the focus area you choose, your overarching goal may be to express yourself with more confidence in six months. Your WHY might be that you desire to have more impact, or you simply want to feel freer and more authentic in your expression. Your measurable steps could be that you start asking for what you want and speaking your truth at company meetings while potentially feeling uncomfortable, or that you start a blog and promote each post on social media, or that you set up informational coffees with three people you admire in the next six months. Some goals—like "feeling more confident"—can be less measurable, but you'll know if the result is achieved if you're feeling and acting differently.

COACHING MOMENT

Why you want the results you're after is important to note for those days when you feel overwhelmed by doing something so challenging. Your WHY is your motivation to keep you going through the arduous moments and dips of enthusiasm.

Once you have an end point for three focus areas, your vision will get more and more clear as you live into it. The work you just did will be your guide.

Future Visions: Don't Worry, Be Happy

"You must give birth to your images. They are the future waiting to be born. Fear not the strangeness you feel. The future must enter into you long before it happens. Just wait for the birth, for the hour of new clarity."

— Rilke

You can only live in the moment and take actions in the now, so your future visions become a guide for your moment-to-moment actions. If your future vision is positive, inspiring, and aligned with your values and ideals, you'll be happy taking steps and being responsible. If, instead, you direct your energy to imagining worrisome future scenarios, such as, "I'll never get a new client again. I'm going to lose my job. What if my house burns down? I'm afraid I'll retire in poverty ..." you will become scared and paralyzed. You cannot fix something that isn't broken. We can handle chaos in the moment but not a made-up scenario in the future. Positive future visions are expansive and inspire actions, worry visions constrict and paralyze.

When you're feeling lost about what to do because you are worried about a made-up scenario, ask yourself: "How can I be responsible for this concern now?" If there is a step you can take right now, do it. For example, if you're worried about your belongings being damaged or stolen, get insurance to cover what concerns you. If you're worried about losing your clients, ask yourself what they might be needing from you that you're not providing. If you're worried about losing your job, ask yourself why and if there's something you can do better. If you're worried about never finding a job in your field, ask yourself something in line with, "Have I reached out to my full network? Who knows something about or someone in the field I'm looking?" And if you ask yourself how you can be responsible for this worry beyond what you're doing now and nothing comes up ... don't worry, keep visioning your ideal future, let that guide you, and be happy.

You now have your life vision, core values, short-term primary focus areas, and goals with measurable results for the next six months. The rest of this book will offer you inspiration, support, and a framework to help make your dreams a reality.

"In every life we have some trouble
But when you worry you make it double
Don't worry
Be happy"

— Bobby McFerrin

PART

TWO

4

YOU'RE
NEVER ALONE

Friends Seen and Unseen

THE WORLD IS A MAGICAL PLACE.

You are never alone. You have people all around you. You can pick up the phone, call a friend, and get together for tea, dinner, or dancing. You can meet with your friends and colleagues and enjoy the energy they exude. You can experience what they uniquely bring out in you, while you laugh and cry together. You can feel human connection any time you look into someone's eyes—whether friend, family, partner, or stranger.

When you have an idea for something new outside of your comfort zone, you don't have to go it alone. You can find a mentor or advisor who has already walked that road and has done something similar. You can work with a coach to help you clarify and put words to your vision, gain more confidence, and start taking those courageous steps forward.

We also have ourselves. When you tap into your creativity, wonder, awe, courage, and brilliance, there is much energy, intuition, and creativity within you to engage and entertain you for hours on end.

In addition, there is an unseen world of energies to draw from. Think of your grandmother who passed, a parent who is no longer with you, a friend who died too young and with whom you enjoyed certain conversations like with no other. If you wish, you can use your imagination and connection, ask for their advice and guidance, and listen to what comes to you. Hold them in your mind's eye and include them at times when you feel their particular essence and their love would be of benefit.

Beyond those you know, who are no longer in the physical world, I believe we have guides and protectors: Angels, God, Goddess, Spirit Guides, Ancient Ones, the Universe... whatever name you want to call these unseen energies is irrelevant. If you ever pray, ask for guidance (talk to the unseen), sit in awe over how a plant grows and blossoms, how our Earth continues to exist, how your child grew through the stages of infancy to adulthood, how you manage to still be alive after the crazy things you've done, you may have an inkling that you're not alone, regardless of how often you tap into this possibility. I gain comfort from my personal experience of feeling never alone, and I trust that more exists beyond what we see—even if what exists is far beyond our current understanding.

There are benefits to removing the veil of separation (sometimes a brick wall of separation) we can create between us and other people in our world and between us and the unseen energies we have access to. People enjoy having friends and feeling wanted, needed, and loved. Being seen and heard by others is an important aspect of life, and we can do the same in return. Yet we make up many things about what others are thinking or about their reality. It's all made up until we actually connect, get curious, and ask.

Do you feel like doing something with a friend but hold back on calling anyone because you assume they are busy and having a fun life without you? If so, you may be making that up! Call and ask if they are available.

Do you care about someone but feel afraid to tell them in case you are rejected? Or maybe you are afraid of what they might think of your crazy honesty. If you're holding back your truth out of fear, then you are the one creating separation and consequently feeling alone. It's practically a mathematical equation. Don't connect = feel alone.

Take this idea and translate it to love relationships, friendships, and connections with classmates and colleagues. Apply this concept to how you show up for phone calls, in-person meetings, networking, interviews, and stage presentations.

The people you want to connect with have their own fears and reasons to create separation, but they also want to feel connected ... so make it easy for them. Reach out your hand for the handshake, make others at the party feel welcomed and comfortable, be the one to invite the new person in the class or on the team to lunch, and help others at the meeting feel heard.

The Gift of Conversation

THERE IS AN ELEMENT OF CONVERSATION THAT IS SACRED AND TRANSCENDS THE WORDS.

Daring leaders have bold ideas that scare them, but when the fear is neutralized through conversation, a reality check, perspective, and laughter ... they are returned to their Joyous Adult self who can be responsible for their dreams and aspirations. The challenge becomes welcomed.

"AS LONG AS YOU'RE IN CONVERSATION, THERE'S HOPE" is something I often mention when my clients are struggling with others. Conversations are not always comfortable, but they are a key form of connection and one of the main tools we have for collaboration.

It's important to get comfortable with expressing yourself, having a debate, even an argument, as long as it's respectful and comes to a clean and gracious close. It's important to ask when you have a question and share your thoughts with your family, friends, and colleagues when you want them to know something. People can't read your mind. Don't live in assumption when by asking questions you can know the truth and the facts.

Communicating effectively is an art we can all learn, practice, and improve upon. Whether you're sitting across from someone, on the telephone, on videoconference, sending an email, or posting on social media, know that your method of communication defines you, and

WHAT COMES OUT OF YOUR MOUTH REFLECTS WHAT'S IN YOUR HEART AND MIND.

Conversations come in many forms some of which are:

- **Intimate sharing** with someone we know well and care about. If you're afraid of intimacy and being open and vulnerable, you'll miss experiencing the gift of this type of conversation.

- **Professional conversations** where you need to create a point of entry so as not to blindside or bulldoze the other. You need to have humility to build trust and to show compassion. First gaining understanding as to what the person(s) can see and align with and then starting the conversation from there will create a successful exchange.

- **Supportive conversations** that we have with friends, family, colleagues, and clients where the goal is to support the other person in every way possible. These require you to be selfless, curious, and focused on the other, and remembering that this is not about you and your wishes but theirs.

- **Conversations that move people** to feel, think, and act in a new way. These conversations can create impact at scale. For this level of conversation, you'll have to find your passion, get the focus off yourself, and remember that your words do have value and can shift a trajectory. You'll want to have your audience front and foremost and consider what exactly they need to hear, what will awaken them, and what will move them.

COACHING MOMENT

The fear that comes with having important conversations expresses a preoccupied focus on self, versus the other. Do you need to get comfortable with intimacy, vulnerability, and having more of you seen? Maybe it's delivery style and curiosity you need to work on. Is it challenging for you to put yourself in another's shoes and listen? Are you remembering that your voice and message is uniquely delivered, and if it moves one person in a sea of people, that matters? Think about what you are specifically afraid of; the awareness alone will make a difference.

Stand in the Other Person's Shoes

Many challenges are created when people don't stop to rise above the circumstances that are confronting or triggering them in relation to another person. Not all circumstances can be risen above, but many can; especially in our response to them. When you don't let go of the story or the thoughts spinning in your head to gain a bit of perspective, when you are stuck in your own story about circumstances, you will miss the gifts that come with the ability to imagine or learn what's going on for the other person.

Before you act based on personal judgment and thinking-you-know, imagine or ask what the other person is experiencing, feeling, and thinking, and consider their motivation. Be curious about the multiple perspectives that are always present. Then, the Joyous Adult you, with love and empathy for yourself and others, can take all into consideration, be discerning, and move forward with humility and inspired action.

When I'm listening to my clients share situations about a difficult relationship, I put myself in their place to understand them, while I simultaneously try to imagine the perspective of the others they are talking about. In doing so, I can rise above the story and bring perspective. When being challenged, we often focus on our feelings and our personal experience. When delivering a message, it is best to process that in advance and spend time focusing on the perspective of the other person, team, or company. Your message will have greater impact when you're honoring yourself, of course, while simultaneously stepping two feet into the other person's shoes.

Make Room for Magic

For the unseen entities in your life, when and how do you connect? Often in fear or distress we send out a random prayer or thought. Think of the last time you were on a turbulent airplane ride. Did thoughts of, "Please keep me safe. Let me live," or "dear god (even if you don't believe in god), please let this be over" trickle through your mind?

Perhaps when things are flowing you don't have the same impulse, but don't you ever feel the synchronicity that seems to be blossoming behind the scenes of your life?

Wow, that was a coincidence.

So easy, just like magic.

I just happened to run into....

I was just thinking of you and your text came in.

I overbooked my day, and someone just rescheduled.

Of course, sometimes things just align nicely, but maybe you can pay attention and play around with synchronicity and coincidence and see if you feel less alone.

THE MAGIC STARTS WHEN YOU CONNECT WITH THESE INCREDIBLE UNSEEN FORCES REGULARLY.

How to stay connected with the unseen energies in your life will be for you to explore and discover, but here are some good avenues: reading passages or tuning into podcasts, videos, etc. from inspirational and/or spiritual leaders you respect. Walking and being in nature. Going to retreats and workshops are common methods. Speaking with a clairvoyant, or using tools like the I Ching, tarot or oracle cards, crystals, and/or runes are options, if you're so inclined. Having a daily ritual like journaling, meditating, reading your core values list, and/or doing a yoga flow can take as little as three minutes or as long as you wish.

I was on a flight from San Francisco to Boston working on the final edits of this book. As I was editing this chapter—the one that makes me feel most vulnerable as an author because I wonder if my readers will think I'm crazy—the woman seated next to me pulled out a handmade booklet titled, in her handwriting, MORNING PRAYERS. I noticed the simply made book was obviously important to her, but I didn't think much of it. I didn't immediately make the connection to what I was editing. So, the Universe got a little louder. She switched books and started reading a book titled Padre Pio by Jose Maria Zavala, with his photo on the cover staring at me. My mother, whom I was on my way to visit, is a devout follower of Padre Pio. She grew up in a small town in Italy a few hours from where this friar and priest, known for his stigmata and mysticism, lived. My mom grew up hearing stories about Padre Pio's miraculous healings from travelers who would stop in her town of Caramanico, Terme, after seeing him in Foggia. My middle name, Pia, honors this priest. Talk about coincidences! It felt to me that unseen forces were at play here: to be on this airplane, editing this book and chapter, and to be sitting next to this woman who went from pulling out her rosaries at the start of the flight, to later moving onto her own "daily ritual" booklet to stay connected to the unseen (right as I was editing the paragraph on the topic), to later pulling out a book that was so connected to my own history. This chapter stays!

Of course, we chatted. I told her my connection to Padre Pio. I gave her the Padre Pio photo I kept in my wallet, knowing my mom would have more for me. Eventually, she asked me what I was writing. I told her about my book, this chapter in particular, and how this encounter was exemplifying it. I can't wait to send her the copy I promised her.

Like you, perhaps, I tend to forget I have a support system when I need them the most, but if I stay connected both to the wonderful people in my life and to the unseen, things are more fun and flow with more ease.

When the World Doesn't Seem Magical

I realize there is a lot out there that's not working, wrong, and outright enraging. Of course, do what you can to change the world for the better, but in the meantime, do not get dragged down by the multitude of events around the globe, and even the galaxy, that our obsession with media gives us access to. If you do, you'll become numb and disconnected from yourself and your immediate environment. Pick your global battles, do the best you can, but first and foremost remember that

THE SMALL ACTS OF LOVE DONE DAILY FOR THE PEOPLE THAT CROSS YOUR PATH WILL HAVE A HUGE RIPPLE EFFECT—SOMETIMES FOR GENERATIONS.

Keep in mind that there are things that come easily to you that are challenging for others. The path you've walked can pave the way for another. Consider being a mentor to someone who could use your support. Be an advocate for someone whose struggle is blindsiding them, and yet, you can see the other side of it. Help someone declutter or design their space, make difficult phone calls, start a dating profile. Write a recommendation. As a result, those you support will move with more spring in their step and go on to bring positivity to others.

COACHING MOMENT

In Chapter 1, you created a list of your core team and your extended network. When you are struggling with a new dream and you feel alone or unsure, go back to that list, and connect with one or two people who can listen to your ideas, your doubts, and advise and support you. Remember that connection is a positive experience not only for you, but for the other person as well. You can also make a regular practice of randomly calling, emailing, or sending a note or a text to people in your life whom you appreciate, for no particular occasion or reason. You will make their day!

5

TWO
FEET IN

Are You Committed?

Indecisiveness is painful, paralyzing, and self-diminishing. Simultaneously, people can have a hard time committing and staying engaged. Commitment feels scary. It triggers the idea that there might be something better out there that we are missing out on, and it stirs our mistrust in others and more importantly ourselves. In addition, when we commit to something new, we face our discomfort with the unknown. There's also the lingering fear of giving it our all and having it not working out.

When we stay in a non-committal state instead of taking steps toward our dream, we hover indecisively on the threshold and never quite make it work.

We don't commit to our relationships, marriages, or jobs; we don't commit to the book we want to write; we don't even commit to our personal mission, passions, or how we want to truly live. We have one foot in and one foot out. We may feel unhappy or directionless, but we let our fear of commitment squash our drive.

When you JUMP IN with two feet, in the pursuit of your ideal life, everything starts to change. You develop the fortitude and personal traits needed to stay focused and thrive.

WITH TWO FEET IN, YOU START TO FEEL IN LOVE WITH WHAT YOU COMMITTED TO.

You see challenges as part of your personal development and know that what you learn along the way will transfer to other aspects of your life. You learn to trust the process of getting over the difficult moments.

Imagine being two feet in your relationship, marriage, where you live, the work you do, the projects you take on, your kids, your friends, the activities you engage in—living a life that reflects joy and fulfillment because you are fully committed to it. You would wake up inspired, passionate, and ready to go each morning.

Put a stake in the ground and two feet in for:

- The larger world and personal world you want to live in
- What you believe is possible and take actions to make it happen
- That project that's been on your back burner a bit too long

- Your children, and those of others, thriving ... as they are our future
- Traveling to that country you want to see
- The fact that you want to learn to knit, dance, sing, snowboard
- The financial future you want to have
- The home you want to live in
- Your alone time
- The baby you desire
- The legacy you want to leave

As an example, I was on the board of a nonprofit that brought art classes to kids in juvenile detention. At one point, the organization was at risk of closing its doors due to lack of funding. I couldn't bear to see the good work of this organization stop after twenty-one years. I jumped two feet in and personally put a stake in the ground saying, "We will not pull art from the kids in juvenile hall. They've had too much removed from their lives already." I honestly had no idea how my vision would manifest, but my passion was enlivened, and I had both feet in, fully committed. After a lot of work, tears, and laughter, and with the support of the board, staff, and donors, the organization was absorbed by a larger nonprofit, and its mission continues and grows. My unwavering commitment was the glue that kept our dream alive, while strategy, consistently showing up, and magical moments of serendipity made it all come together.

In the early years of our marriage, every time my husband and I got into an argument, I would think, "I'm out of here." One foot was always out the door. At one point, I put two feet inside the door, so each little argument didn't upset the apple cart. I realized that the grass may be different and maybe even greener but not necessarily better elsewhere. When you are committed, you stay in to have a discussion and find resolution. You're accepting of differences. You work through challenging moments. You focus your attention on the bigger goals and dreams, and your mind doesn't wander anymore, which helps you create a more powerful relationship (or business, or project, or whatever outcome you're looking for).

You may have friends who are fully committed to their dream of having a child, but their circumstances won't allow that to happen naturally. How many adoptions, surrogate births, and in vitro pregnancies are happening because future parents are ready to have a baby, one way or the other? They are two feet in, regardless of how they get there.

Many of my executive clients have left secure jobs and moved to another organization or started their own company, because they are fully committed to having the impact they truly want to have in the world. **Daring Leaders with Bold Ideas are two feet in**, focused on honoring all their values and overall vision. It's the stake in the ground for their WHY (their key motivation and purpose) that they allow to matter. Now, they have scaled their impact, their values are honored, and their work and lifestyle match their desires and vision.

In my *Ten Day Launchpad* program, the emerging leaders that I work with don't want to be in jobs that leave them feeling unfulfilled. They are proactive and work with me in advance of their first or next job. In the program, they take time to explore what really matters to them and then apply for and get jobs (or launch their own work projects) that are in alignment with their values. Their new work gives them the opportunity to develop professionally and thrive financially while feeling more joyful as they build their career.

When you are inspired and internally driven with a clear mission and commitment, it's like you're putting a stake in the ground and stating to yourself and to all around you, "This is what I'm going to make happen. Are you with me?" That stake and all it stands for becomes what you hold onto in the turbulence of creating change.

COACHING MOMENT

In Chapter 3, you decided on your Primary Focus areas and goals for the next six months and WHY these goals are important. What you put a stake in the ground for is this WHY, the motivation portion of your commitment. That's what you hold onto when the going gets rough. Experiences connected to your deep commitment are so powerful they replace fear with inspired action.

You might fail, but you'll learn in the process, and you will feel and be better because of your willingness to put two feet in and give it your all.

WHEN YOU GIVE IT YOUR ALL, YOU'LL BE DRIVEN BY PASSION, AND YOU'RE VERY LIKELY TO SUCCEED. GO FOR IT!

Step Out from the Shadow of Fear

Are you living in the shadow of fear?

Fear of failure,
Fear of success,
Fear because of past experiences,
Fear of the future you are imagining,
Fear of being judged,
Fear of being loved,
Fear of never finding love,
Fear of being relied upon,
Fear of commitment,
Fear that your ideas have no value,
Fear that no one wants or needs what you have to offer,
Fear of _____.

Yet, every day you get up and go, and depending on your state of mind, you either manage the fears, work to overcome them, or—in the ideal scenario—you take steps forward to acknowledge them while shifting your relationship to them, so they have no impact on your desired outcomes.

When you step out from the shadow of fear and put your stake in the ground for where you're going next, you feel inspired and empowered. You build momentum because you have passion driving you. You build the foundation for more great change, and when it feels turbulent, you circle back to your clear mission, remember your stake, and reconnect to it.

By neutralizing your fear, and stepping out from under its shadow, you glow and become a light for others.

COACHING MOMENT

Do you have a stake in the ground for something you will give your best energy to over the next few months? Something where trying and giving it your all is the only option?

If not, pause and consider—why not?

I'm sure you have dreams. Why not put a stake in the ground for the very outcome YOU DESIRE most?

Think about and answer:

What do you secretly desire and long for?

How will you feel if you never get to this desire?

How will you feel if you try your best and fail?

How will you feel if you try your best and succeed?

Who is one person you can share this dream with?

What would it look and feel like if you put a stake in the ground for this dream goal?

What's one tiny step you can take to move your dream forward?

The Paralysis of Perfectionism

The pursuit of perfectionism can be as paralyzing as fear. For those of you who recognize your own perfectionistic tendencies, know that a more productive aim would be excellence. Whether you're having guests for dinner or starting a company, perfectionism will slow you down and keep you in a mode of indecision and inaction.

The issue is that **perfectionists set a high bar, but as they work to achieve their goal, they keep moving the bar higher**, so the end is never in sight. There's always another tweak to improve the outcome. There is sometimes no end or accomplishment if the perfectionist doesn't let go and surrender. I often tell perfectionists to aim for eighty percent, knowing that will be more than good enough.

Your Love, Your Focus, Your Attention

Everything you choose to do and not do matters. Where you put your love, your focus, and your attention has a ripple effect. What you nurture grows.

Where is your love, focus, and attention going? Is it aligned with your bigger vision and values? If not, what needs to adjust?

Do you get thrown off and give too much weight and focus to circumstances? Do you have thoughts such as: If the circumstances would change, everything would be better?

If I were acknowledged, worked somewhere else, got a raise, was promoted, had more money, had a partner, didn't have a partner my life would be better. Is your upbringing and history the issue? Perhaps it's the many distractions out there, the boredom, or being too busy—all of which can be a part of the endless list of circumstances that you imagine having no control over. Do you tend to look outside of yourself and blame others for how things turn out or how things are going? Each time you argue, is the issue the other person's fault? When you get laid off, is it your supervisor or the company's fault?

If you are an adult and are blaming your lack of success, commitment, and forward movement on something or someone outside of yourself, you need to stop. Consider the circumstance for a moment, and ask, "How am I creating or allowing this to happen?" Just like you create the amazing outcomes in your life, you are also connected to the less exciting outcomes. You give your power away when you give it to someone or something outside of yourself.

Sometimes misfortune strikes. The unexpected happens. Again, you have an opportunity in these cases to assess the issue, and instead of focusing on the misfortune, turn your focus to your response. If it's a deeply emotional response, turning your focus to your emotions and processing your feelings versus the situation will be healing.

COACHING MOMENT

Where are you looking outside of yourself and blaming others or the circumstances as an excuse for your lack of success, commitment, or forward movement? It's not other people or circumstances that stop you.

Once you are ready to stop looking outside of yourself for the answers and have cleared the way for your own power, I really want to ask you one of my favorite coaching questions:

WHERE DO YOU WANT TO PUT YOUR LOVE, YOUR FOCUS, AND YOUR ATTENTION?

Take a breath and take some time to reflect; look back at your Wheel of Life, your Core Values, Primary Focus Areas, and what you're personally passionate about. Really consider what matters to you, what success you envision, and what impact you want to have.

I can almost guarantee that when you give less weight to the current circumstances, clarify your vision, and choose where YOU want to put your LOVE, FOCUS, and ATTENTION everything will start to change. First, inside you, since you will connect to your power, passion, and purpose—which is where all change starts—and then slowly your future circumstances will change to align with what's currently within you.

I see this happening all the time with my clients. They start a coaching relationship with a desire to create change and, at some level, lack clarity and courage. As they start to answer the question "where do you want to put your love, your focus, and your attention," the answers to where, who, and what start to reveal themselves. Often, the answer is right under their nose; they don't have to look long or far. Trust yourself; **start aligning your internal world and your external world will align with you**.

ENJOY LIVING LIFE WITH TWO FEET IN.

6

EMBRACING
CHAOS

The Gifts of Chaos

CHAOS IS THE DOORWAY TO CHANGE.

It doesn't have to be trauma-producing chaos, but some level of mess or emotional discomfort often precedes positive change. The key is, once again, to step right into the chaos and engage fully (another opportunity to put both feet in). The more you push it away the longer it will linger.

When people think of chaos, they tend to think of turbulent times that aren't as easy as they prefer. Chaos isn't always negative, but it typically creates drama and added activity. Chaos can also come in various forms, such as chaos in your home or other environment (e.g., a pipe breaks behind your wall, floods the kitchen, and suddenly you need mold remediation and an unplanned remodel). Physical chaos is when something is not right with your body and there's physical vulnerability. Emotional chaos is when you experience loss, trauma, and emotional pain. Chaos can affect the various areas of your Wheel of Life such as your Career, your Finances, your Friends & Community, your Family, and even your Spirituality.

Chaos can be planned or unplanned. If you want to rearrange a room, you'll move things around, empty closets, and make a mess to get to your ideal: a room that matches your needs and aesthetics. That's planned chaos.

Being suddenly let go from a job creates unexpected chaos. It's like having the rug pulled out from under you. Often, however, once you get back up on your feet, you realize that you stayed at the old job for security and comfort, but you didn't fully love it. You set to the task of finding a new job that's more aligned to your skills and passions.

Once, I traveled with my husband, my two young boys, and my mom to enjoy her hometown of birth in Italy. One hour before leaving the town, my mother fell and her femur broke. Instead of heading to Rome to continue our vacation, we headed to the closest hospital. Mom needed surgery, followed by a month of rehabilitation. That certainly created unexpected chaos! We had to devise alternative plans on the spot. My husband and kids went on to Rome, and I stayed behind. Suddenly, I was no longer a tourist, and I got to spend a week as a resident in my mom's hometown before settling her into a rehabilitation home for a month of care. I had a magical experience being in her town to manage on my own. I called it the City of Angels, because I felt always supported. And, over the course of a month, my mom got to spend hours being loved by her childhood friends, as they all visited her in rehab as she healed, perhaps from more than just her surgery.

Another time, my doctor informed me that I needed surgery, it should happen in one month, and I would be in the hospital for a week. I was scared for my family and myself. After the initial shock, I became very curious: What lessons were in this for me? Why … me, this, now? As I started to share my dilemma with my closest circle of friends, I found myself creating a small team to support me emotionally and my family logistically, and I embraced the physical, emotional, and spiritual chaos I was suddenly in. After doing all my research and looking into and trying alternative healing options, I committed to the surgery. In the end, I had an extraordinary view from my hospital room; the wide windowsill was filled with flowers from friends and family. I gained a huge respect for nurses and what they do, and I let myself be taken care of. I was in awe that acquaintances, who were not initially on my radar as potential sources of support, offered to help my family and me. The gift and silver lining in this chaos was the love I received. I realized that I was loved in a way I didn't understand before. That realization was the doorway to change for me. That feeling of all the love coming my way, like a wave washing over me, has stayed with me to this day. When I feel self-doubt, I can remember that feeling of being loved by so many people who I didn't know cared about me, and trust that if they cared then, so must the people who surround me now. It puts my concerns in a new light.

Chaos, whether expected or not, often comes bearing gifts. I encourage you to slow down and acknowledge them. Doing so will bring meaning to the most vulnerable of times.

Let's face it, life is complex, crap happens, and there's often something that feels chaotic to varying degrees. Practice letting those times become the undercurrents in a sea where you are calm. Life can be great and simultaneously turbulent. Don't dwell on the ups and downs. Stay above them. Stay buoyed by surrounding yourself with people who are creative thinkers, solution-oriented, visionary, and look for opportunities and meaning—not problems; you'll stay much calmer and manage the turbulence as a side activity.

IMAGINING CHAOS IN YOUR FUTURE IS PARALYZING AND FRIGHTENING. YET, MANAGING CHAOS AS IT'S HAPPENING IS EMPOWERING.

As you realize how innately capable you are, your courage grows, you gain confidence, and you realize you can manage chaos. Walking through times of chaos and seeing the resulting benefits is one of the ways you'll learn the process involved with creating change. Walking through that process and coming out whole on the other side of it teaches you what you are made of and builds your courage and self-esteem, all while tapping into your humility. Any time you show up for yourself, do what you say you're going to do, and walk through a metaphorical fire, you realize more of your potential. Each time you make your way through a chaotic time, you learn more about your capacity to manage whatever comes your way.

I personally treasure experiences that humble and strengthen, make me laugh, make me cry, and elicit the full range of my humanness.

Remember, chaos is the doorway to change, so sometimes we consciously or unconsciously create it to shake things up, and other times we simply choose to manage it when it presents itself. Like with everything in life, the more you engage and see the positive results, the more your capacity grows, and the less dramatic chaotic times become.

The Shadow Side of Chaos

If you are someone who moves from one drama to the next, in a turmoil of tension and stress, you may ask yourself if you are addicted to chaos. Think about it: What are you getting out of it? Perhaps attention, camaraderie, and helpers surrounding you? Possibly, the chaos life throws your way becomes an excuse for why you can't get to the things that matter most to you, the reason for your failings. This is a form of powerlessness and blame. Or is chaos the way you get your adrenalin to flow? You end up with energy but then don't apply it to what's creating the commotion. What is the noise allowing you to avoid? If you're drowning in internal or external chaos, you might be avoiding something more emotionally challenging and/or you may have a fear of change. You are probably not imagining or realizing that there are gifts around the corner waiting for you.

Here are places to look for chaos addiction: your finances (you're behind on bookkeeping, taxes, bill paying, work stability, and income); your relationships (constant arguments and turmoil with your parents, siblings, partner, colleagues, and friends); your schedule (too booked, overwhelmed, not enough time); your health (less than vibrant, not at your ideal weight, physical weakness at a young age, unmanaged health issues); your physical environment (clutter, dirty, constantly misplacing objects, or simply not the way you really want it to be).

Refer back to each section of the Wheel of Life, and ask yourself: Is there chaos here now or do I foresee it coming? What step can I take to mitigate, eliminate, or manage it? Seeing chaos and stepping in to address it will create change and provide gifts you cannot yet imagine.

Why Me?

When presented with a challenging situation, wiping away the "W-h-y MEEEE?" asked out of self-pity and replacing it with, "Hmmm, why me?" elicits curiosity, learning, expansion, and growth.

Try, "Hmmmm...Why is this showing up in my life now? What is it trying to teach me?" Get curious and your situation will take a turn for the positive.

When chaos belongs to you or is in your life, don't skirt it or dance around it. Go right in and embrace it courageously. If it's not your chaos, you can choose if you want to support it, be a part of it, and/or let it ride its course without your involvement. Sometimes, you may choose to simply observe it, allowing those to which it belongs to learn and grow from it, as they will.

COACHING MOMENT

Life can get messy. Here is my quick "chaos formula" to help you deal with it:

- Keep both feet in.

- Keep the end goal in mind.

- Remember the universe has your back. (If you don't believe in that, find a friend or two who have your back during a particularly chaotic time.)

- Take the very next step to keep moving forward through the chaos.

- Look for the gifts.

7

WALKING WITH
UNCERTAINTY

Being Human

Something that consistently amazes me is that we humans have the courage to dream of all we want to be, do, and achieve; we design our lives accordingly and take steps towards our optimal future... all while walking side-by-side with uncertainty daily.

In our strength, we are inspired to shift, change, and grow as we engage with life, all the time knowing that the rug can be pulled out from under us. We can literally or metaphorically trip and fall. A myriad of things can happen to us or to those we love that divert our plans. Yet, through our many life experiences, the courage and incredible fortitude we have is revealed. This is the crazy dichotomy of having a human experience.

Mostly unconsciously, the one choice we are making daily is to live. From that basic choice, step-by-step, we can lift our lives to levels we ourselves cannot fathom on our path to realizing our full potential—actualizing ourselves. At our best, we care for ourselves, are of service to our family, friends, and complete strangers. We express ourselves freely and authentically.

With this said, UNCERTAINTY walks along with us. The truth is a bus could hit you, you could get cancer, or have a ski accident. The economy could crash and mess up your plans. Your company could have massive layoffs, you might get fired, or your business could fail. A loved one may die, turning your life upside down. As we've seen, there could even be a global pandemic. There are many ways for the rug to get pulled out from under us.

It's not that I want to put these negative scenarios out there for you to fear. My point is that

WE ARE INCREDIBLY POWERFUL, COURAGEOUS, AND RESILIENT BEINGS. WE MUST EMBODY THIS TRUTH AND BELIEVE IT TO THE CORE OF OUR BEING, because each day, as we live, love, design our future, move forward through our challenges, and heal ourselves, we know that if the rug gets pulled out from under us, we'll trip, fall, and get up again.

This concept became very clear to me, and a part of my personal framework, after my dear friend died of cancer at the young age of 52. She was a distinguished jewelry designer, and although ill for a few years, lived her life fully until the very end. Two days before passing, she was still carving wax for a ring design at her kitchen table. Yes, her life was shorter than she or anyone had hoped for, but she lived it without letting the cancer stop her dreams or diminish her dynamic energy. She continued to engage with her loved ones, employees, and clients. She left a beautiful legacy for many who knew her, own her pieces, or continue to make jewelry in her style, and especially for those of us who had the privilege to share life, conversations, perspectives, and even her passing with her.

COACHING MOMENT

I have the deepest belief in your capacity to live powerfully, joyfully, and successfully. I know you can be, do, and have all that you focus on creating while allowing uncertainty to walk by your side. If you embrace this perspective, it will empower you to realize that you are already capable and have the courage to move past the potential challenges life may present. This innate partnership with uncertainty makes the rest child's play.

Focus on the Present

Newsfeeds and other media can instill a sense of instability and even panic into our lives. Besides the stories coming from outside of us, we often make things up in our head to worry about. When we envision scenarios about the future that end poorly, we walk around feeling anxious as a result. We scare ourselves.

Fearing uncertainty about the future can keep you from being your true self. Fearing uncertainty keeps us from actualizing ourselves individually and as a collective humanity. In the present, you can't do anything about these made-up scenarios, yet they keep you restricted and timid. You can't be bold and daring when you're paralyzed by uncertainty.

We all have times when we create negative future scenarios. This is not useful. The most empowering images to create in your mind are of the positive outcomes you are working towards. In the meantime, here are some pointers for addressing the worry.

COACHING MOMENT

Think about the specific outcome you are worried about.
Then ask yourself: How can I be responsible for this today? Is there anything I need to do now?

Examples:
If you're imagining personal belongings or work equipment being stolen or your house burning down and losing it all ...

Ask: How can I be responsible for this today? Is there anything I need to do now?

Possible answer/action: I can call an insurance agent and make sure I have the proper coverage for the specifics I'm concerned about.

If you're imagining running out of money and being unsuccessful or homeless in your old age …

Ask: How can I be responsible for this today? Is there anything I need to do now?

Possible answer/action, depending on your age and where you are in your career:

- Use your network, be clear on what you offer, and promote your services (adjust this to your line of work).

- Schedule a meeting with your trusted financial planner. If you don't have one, schedule consultations with three advisers as a starter. Listen to what they have to say and take some new actions in the present to protect yourself from your feared future scenario.

- Create a spreadsheet of your inflows and outflows and do the math. Become familiar with where there are financial gaps and act responsibly to move towards your dream scenario.

If the economy is in a low point and you're afraid of losing your customers ...

Ask: What do my clients specifically need now? Are there problems I can help them with? How can I better serve them? What can I give them to ease this time for them?

Possible answer/action, depending on your own scenario:

- You can offer bonus add-ons to their time with you.

- You can offer special pricing for a limited time.

- Your clients might appreciate it if you, or your team, reach out to them individually to simply check in and give them the best individualized service anyone can imagine.

- You can maintain their trust by showing compassion, being a stable entity during a rough patch, and giving them hope for the future.

- You can take extremely good care of your mind, body, and spirit, and keep your own energy high, so you can provide your best level of service.

WHEN YOU EMBRACE AND INTEGRATE THAT YOU'VE BEEN
WALKING SIDE BY SIDE WITH UNCERTAINTY SINCE THE
DAY YOU WERE BORN, YOU WILL START TO RECOGNIZE
YOUR POWER AND TRUST YOURSELF IN THIS INTIMATE
LIFELONG RELATIONSHIP.

_8

TRUST

Operating Instructions

Over and over again, your inner voice (or however your thoughts and ideas come to you) will tell you exactly what you need to do. You will get what I call "operating instructions." These typically provide direction on a step to take in relationship to something you want to manifest. My own operating instructions come in the form of a voice telling me what step to take, but you may see a clear vision or have a strong feeling. You may find that your operating instructions don't always make sense or seem to align with your ultimate desire. That's because the operating instructions may only be giving you the v-e-r-y next step. You can only take one step at a time, so sometimes that is all you are given. What needs to follow is a leap of faith on your behalf and a deep trust in your own inner guidance system.

When you learn to hear and trust the internal messages related to your current challenge or feeling of being stuck, you'll thrive.

AS YOU GAIN CLARITY ON WHAT YOU WANT TO MANIFEST AS YOUR ULTIMATE GOAL, THE HOW WILL REVEAL ITSELF.

You will learn to trust this process, but the very first step—your operating instructions from me to you—is to become aware of these messages that are guiding you towards your desired outcomes.

I coined the term "operating instructions" in relationship to the inner guidance I received in my third year of being a trained coach. At that time, I had finished my coaching certification, and I had helped a good number of clients, but they were all completing their coaching time with me. I was down to three clients, and I feared that I would soon have only two, and in my mind, that could no longer be considered a business. I had just done a few complimentary consultations, which often lead to new clients. Although they were with people I would have enjoyed working with and could support, they all said they couldn't afford the coaching.

I sat one day feeling distressed, afraid that my passion career would end, and not knowing what to do to grow my business. In that moment, my inner voice spoke to me and said: *Open three scholarship spots at whatever fee potential clients can afford.* That message came as a shock since it was against logic. I tried to argue, get more information, but that was all I got, and the message had been crystal clear. My goal at the time was to get to ten full-paying clients! How was this going to help me reach it?

After taking a breath, I decided that I would open three scholarship spots in my roster of ten ideal clients. I called back the clients who said they couldn't afford it, letting them know of my new scholarship openings. One said she would love the coaching and could pay ... an amount so low I never would have imagined it. I gulped and said yes. She turned out to be an amazing client for me to work with.

Eventually, I did build my client roster to ten full-paying clients and beyond, and I've continued to offer scholarship opportunities ever since. At the time, what I was given was only the very next step, not the full strategy, but even though I didn't understand how it could help me, I took a leap of faith and heeded the message. That first scholarship client ended up being a treasure in that I learned as much from our every conversation as she gained from the coaching. I refined my skills, experienced more of my own power as a coach, and therefore projected more confidence, which helped me gain more clients. Over the years, my scholarship clients have shown up fully, and, like all my clients, have realized more of their own potential. Experiencing that as a coach is priceless.

Over the years, I've learned to trust my operating instructions.

MIRACLES HAPPEN WHEN YOU LIVE IN EASE AND TRUST, WITH HOPE AND EXPECTATION FOR A POSITIVE OUTCOME.

Appreciate the moments in your day when there's serendipity and coincidence. Notice when the going gets rough and you know you need a miracle—it comes. Be open to receiving the magic, and be grateful each and every time. Eventually, you'll build a relationship with your inner guidance, and you will TRUST its messages and allow them to grow stronger. That message from my inner voice really was an everyday miracle.

Change Happens Over Time

I used to be a professional clothing designer and have always been surrounded by creatives: artists, chefs, writers, filmmakers, and designers of all sorts. What I learned from being a designer and maker is that creating something from nothing takes time.

An overnight success is never what it seems. People in leadership positions or in places of high visibility didn't get there as quickly as it may appear. The process of creating—including creating changes in your life or in society—happens over an arc of time. Listen to the story of anyone who has built a successful life, business, career, relationship, product, invention, or has worked to create system changes, and you'll hear stories of trials, persistence, and patience.

The key to those successes is **PASSION**, **ENTHUSIASM**, **WILLINGNESS**, **HOPE**, and **COMMITMENT** when the going gets rough, **CONSISTENCY** in taking steps towards your goal, and **TRUST** that time is on your side. Additionally, getting comfortable with learning as you go, the many moments you'll be uncomfortable, and accepting that nothing is guaranteed.

One sign of a leader is when someone is comfortable consistently being outside of their comfort zone. A leader is always at the forefront of uncharted territory, going where others have not gone in their actions or thinking, and bringing others along. Think of a leader you admire; and learn how long it took them to reach success and how passion, enthusiasm, willingness, hope, commitment, consistency, and trust were present in their stories.

Over time, your vision will clarify, you'll master how to achieve what you want, responsibilities will increase and diminish, and your relationship to time will change. People will notice your solidity, opportunities will cross your path, and you'll know which to seize. With time, and each step you take towards creating increments of success, your confidence builds, momentum builds, and then POP ... it happens. You're in a new reality, seemingly overnight. And from that new place, your foundation is stronger, and you can build even more of what you want moving forward.

I hold onto this framework that **change happens over time** in my own life, as I watch my children, now young men, evolve and shape their futures. With each new client, I know change will happen over the time of our coaching relationship and in increments with each call or meeting. I'm always curious and ever trusting of this unfolding. Coaching is a process that happens over time, and in that framework, internal transformation and incredible changes can take place.

COACHING MOMENT

Some thoughts to hold onto when your momentum has come to a halt:

- Are you clear on your vision, and are your words and actions in alignment with what you want?

Notice if you are giving yourself and others mixed messages. If you are, you cannot expect to achieve a desired outcome. If you're not quite clear on what you want to achieve, I'm sure you're clear on what you do not want. Don't take any actions leading you towards what you know you don't want or speak of what you do not want as if you want it.

Example of misaligned words and desires: Single people that deeply want a life partner saying: *I love my freedom, having the bed all to myself, and my peaceful living space. I don't want to give that up.* That's a mixed message unless you truly want a life partner and two homes—which you might. Whatever it is, be sure your words and actions are in alignment.

Clarity and alignment will lead to feeling passion, enthusiasm, willingness, and hope in relation to your vision—which will lead to your commitment and consistency in taking steps.

Time Is On Your Side

When things take longer than anticipated, there's often something better being conjured up. See for yourself, if in the process of creating what you wanted, the outcome turned out better than anticipated because of some glitch or slowdown that happened along the way.

Think back to times when you were trying to move forward and there were unexpected delays. Did you later meet a new person who was the ideal connection? Did a new technology develop, making your life easier? Did you get a great discount or find a better price after having missed the first opportunity to buy something you needed?

When my husband and I wanted to buy a house in San Francisco, it took us four years and bidding on five properties we thought were wonderful before winning the bid on the home we live in. We never wavered in our passion and commitment to own a home and what our dream home should look like. When a house that was ideal for our family hit the market, we had mastered bidding in a competitive market, and got it.

Another example of time being on my side is that any time I have an overloaded day, a client will coincidently need to shift their call to another day. Sometimes, I want a client to shift their time, but I typically don't even ask, since they most likely will shift it themselves. I remain in awe and trust that time works with me and not against me.

Trust Yourself

What's the smallest step you can take towards your desired outcome? We can only take one step at a time. Sometimes we're in the flow, and we move so fast that our steps take on a jogging or sprinting pace, and other times, we're paralyzed. In those moments, instead of freezing up, ask: **What's the smallest step I can take? Then take it.**

I have wanted to write a book for years. I thought about it, talked about it on occasion, made some notes, but I was paralyzed in starting. Not until I took the smallest baby steps could I build momentum, fall in love with my project, and make my dream a reality.

First, I started by committing to going to a café a few mornings per week and writing. After I did that a few times, I trusted myself to follow through on that step. Then I floundered around trying to shape an outline and decided I would just keep showing up at the café, write whatever was on my mind, and make an outline later. That worked. Showing up for my project allowed me to get into it, find my way, trust myself, and finally get it to a point where I could start asking for help to bring it over the finish line.

Trusting yourself is foundational. Whether with yourself or another, you build trust by being reliable, dependable, keeping promises, showing up, and being consistent. When you exhibit these characteristics by keeping the promises you make to yourself, you build your own self-esteem. When you are trustworthy with others, this allows for dynamic and meaningful relationships. Your life journey is likely to be enjoyable when you trust yourself, trust time, and listen to your own operating instructions!

GRATITUDE &
CELEBRATION

"Gratitude is a spontaneous celebration of love, joy, vulnerability, thankfulness, and surrender."

— Lazaris

Celebration Expands

I often ask my clients to imagine what they want to feel grateful for and want to be celebrating at the end of the year on December 31. Their visions, steeped in desire, guide our work. Once you get to the end of the year or the end of a project, it's important to pause and truly celebrate all of it, feel the love you gave, the joy you felt, the vulnerability of not knowing, your commitment to keep going, the thankfulness towards others you partnered with and toward yourself—along with the surrender in giving it your all. Celebrating your own accomplishments and acknowledging how you have been changed because of all you have received and given nurtures your spirit. It expands your capacity to receive more as you move forward.

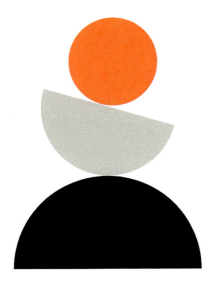

Gratitude Transforms

When children take their first steps, we cheer and make it obvious that we are celebrating them and their accomplishment. We celebrate the successes of colleagues, friends, and relatives, as well as the wins of teams and athletes we know and don't know. We express gratitude for gifts others bring us, and we show appreciation for the people who work with us and support us. Expressing gratitude for others reinforces your connections, completes a circle of exchange, and allows your joy to expand. There's good reason why giving flower bouquets and sending thank you notes have been popular since the Middle Ages.

The other point about gratitude is that you can't always return a favor to those who've helped you. Often, you must simply receive, and when you're fully nurtured, you will give to many others someday, somehow. **The act of giving is joyous and fulfilling on its own; in many cases, we never need to receive from those to whom we've given, since the opportunity to give and contribute to someone else's life is the gift**. Giving and receiving is not always reciprocal or equal and it absolutely doesn't need to be. That's where deep gratitude will fill the void that you cannot fill by actions of doing and giving. In essence, gratitude is about acknowledging who another person was for you or how a circumstance turned out, and simultaneously, who you were being in the situation. Moments of gratitude are deeply intimate and transformative.

It's important to pause when you've attained success, reached a goal, had a miracle happen, received kindness, and/or were able to impact the life of another through your actions. It's important to reflect and celebrate the circumstances, serendipity, and most of all, who you were being.

Instead of glossing it all over and moving on, learn how to feel deeply and acknowledge all involved, including yourself. With how many friends, colleagues, and family members do you share the beauty you see, the gratitude you feel, the accomplishments you are making, the success you are having … through words, pictures, and small gifts?

Have your moments and allow yourself to be boastful with dear friends, family, and colleagues, and celebrate your accomplishments with glee. That will give them room to do the same with you when they're feeling proud. In the evening, be grateful for your day and know that you did enough.

If you are always running a race with no opportunity to cross a finish line, throw your arms up in joy, feel gratitude, and celebrate your success ... you will not enjoy the journey. Your spirit will not want to keep playing along with this type of torture!

IT'S OUR CHOICE TO CELEBRATE AND FEEL DEEP GRATITUDE FOR EACH UNIQUE EXPERIENCE.

Yet, we often have a harder time gratefully acknowledging our own accomplishments. If that's true for you, pause to consider why. Perhaps you consistently diminish yourself, what you do, and have to say thereby shrinking your own value. Perhaps you were raised to be humble, not prideful, and confuse that with being proud and celebrating. Humility and pride can co-exist. Perhaps your parents taught you not to be boastful, and now you have stopped celebrating yourself. Were you raised in a home where perfection was the driver, and perhaps you were constantly being told how you could improve? And there's always the feeling of not having reached the ever elusive "enough," and therefore, you're fixated on the next goal and always running a race with no end.

If your reluctance to celebrate your accomplishments has to do with your childhood history, remember that you are no longer living in that past reality. You have a nurturing voice within you now, that can celebrate you and others and feel gratitude for your being and your life.

WITH ALL THE VOICES WITHIN YOU, CAN YOU CHOOSE TO LISTEN TO THE MOST NURTURING INNER VOICE?

COACHING MOMENT

Recall some of your most recent accomplishments, large or small. When you accomplish a successful day's work, complete a large project, or give someone assistance that makes their life easier do you pause to have GRATITUDE for YOUR own accomplishments?

Do you stop and CELEBRATE with yourself and others the great thing you did today, this week, this month, or this year? Do you pause to consider who you had to BE to accomplish your desired end goal?

If you just keep pressing forward, and don't stop to feel gratitude for your big and small accomplishments and the life you have created to date, you will be ignoring and diminishing yourself. That is mean! Why would you want to move forward with new desires and projects, when you already know you won't stop and feel the gratitude and deeply celebrate the truth of who you are and what you've done? Parts of you will resist the abuse of doing without any celebration and gratitude, and your progress will be stunted.

Take some time to think back over your past week—is there anything you feel proud of, excited about, and in essence, grateful for? Think back over the past three to six months and do the same.

Gratitude is an emotional experience. Allow yourself to be moved by gratitude. Consider what it would be like for a child to take a first step, say a first word, write a first letter, give a hug, and/or say, "I love you" without you feeling the GRATITUDE and CELEBRATING the moment.

When we don't acknowledge and celebrate ourselves we can feel empty and depleted. We then look outside of ourselves for what we are truly meant to give to ourselves. We start looking outside of ourselves for acknowledgements, awards, promotions, another degree, and for love—but we do it out of the fear that if we don't have and do more and climb higher, we'll have no value and be left feeling empty. It is necessary to remember that **the only one who can truly fill you is you**. When you start with gratitude and acknowledgment for yourself and your life, then all those outside rewards will be joyous to receive but not needed to fill any internal voids.

BEFORE you embark on any doing or achieving, be sure to connect to your gratitude for the opportunities and for the outcomes you're going to create. Celebrate your courage and who you are at the core and be prepared to pause and celebrate the smaller markers of success along the way.

COACHING MOMENT

Think of the upcoming events, experiences, and achievements that you already know your organization, business, family, and friends will have in the coming months. Plan on embracing them and being fully present for them. Talk about them in advance, make room for them on your calendar, turn them into group celebrations, plan ahead, and create ways to make them even more remarkable and celebratory. You can feel gratitude that they are in your future before the moment arrives.

Mirror, Mirror

In our most vibrant years, we constantly look in the mirror and self-criticize. We compare and contrast and wish something were different. Unfortunately, this typically happens throughout life, but it's especially painful to watch young people in their most vibrant, strong, energetic years hold back when in fact their vibrancy, innocence, creativity, and courage is what's compelling and needed.

How many times have you looked back at old photos to see how beautiful you were, yet continue to look in the mirror and criticize? Repeating the cycle, six months or years later, looking back only to see your beauty in the past tense. What if you saw, appreciated, and celebrated your beauty today? What if you saw yourself through the lens of love, the way you look at children, your friends, and so many others? What if you turned those loving eyes, appreciation, and gratitude towards yourself?

You can transform your experience by consistently filling your own well and by being in constant GRATITUDE and CELEBRATION for your life, your unique expression, and what you do and bring. Honor both what you fail and succeed at. Have GRATITUDE and CELEBRATION for the journey as well as the outcomes.

_10

YOUR LEGACY

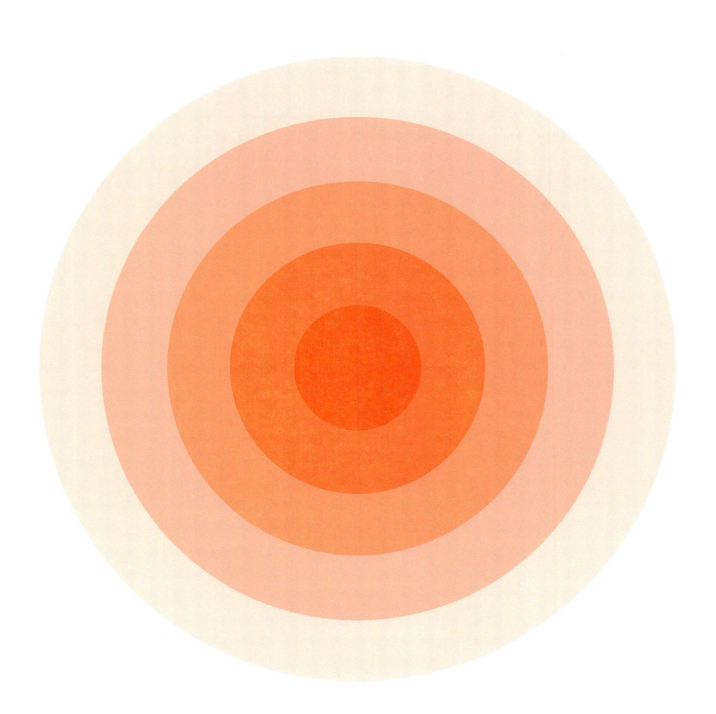

A Mission-Driven Life

Legacy, being of service, kindness to others, and abundance of resources are all interconnected and reflect a mission-driven life.

Everything you do or don't do has an impact. This isn't meant to add pressure, but awareness. Not attending an event has a different impact than if you do attend. One choice is not better than another, but it does have an effect on you and other people.

YOUR CHOICES ARE KEY AND THE PRIMARY STEPPING-STONES THAT ADD UP TO THE LIFE YOU LIVE AND LEGACY YOU LEAVE.

Typically, we think of a legacy as leaving to others money, personal property, teachings, information, intellectual property, inventions, creations, values, and impact that will live on at the familial, organizational, national, or global scale after we are gone.

We tend to think of legacy as something positive that we leave behind; and hopefully it is, but don't be fooled thinking a negative impact and footprint doesn't ripple on as we age or after we've departed. Just think of the positive and negative impact your parents, siblings, and teen friends have had on you. Some you've celebrated and appreciated, and the rest you've had to process, work through, and let go of over the years.

We all leave a legacy. We will impact many during our lifetime, and we will be remembered. We all leave a money legacy—whether it's positive, negative, or unremarkable; some objects—whether appreciable, discardable, useful, or mementos; and we will leave an impression on the lives of others and our planet.

Your awareness, forethought, intentions, choices, and actions today and in the years to come matter. They will impact how you and your generations of peers are remembered and what impact you have on other people, places, nature, and animals. It's not easy, when in your teens and young adult years, to think about the impact of actions long into the future, but it shows a tremendous awareness to do so.

COACHING MOMENT

Take time to gain a high-level view of your life now. Does it impact your circle of people and the bigger world in ways that matter to you? What is the ripple effect of your actions today? To do this, you could return to the Wheel of Life, and look to see what you wrote about your life now and your vision for it. Look with curiosity if some of those current truths or ideal visions will leave a positive impact on your family, community, our planet, and/or society. What's the footprint and legacy you are creating through your own future vision of your life?

Living your life with a mission to create positive impact brings joy and satisfaction like nothing else. It helps you grow to actualize as much of your potential as is possible. Simultaneously, it also helps you to succeed. When you think bigger and beyond your own needs, it takes your focus off what people are thinking of you and puts your attention on what you are trying to achieve for others. Focusing outward gives us the gumption to be courageous and determined and think bigger and beyond our own needs.

Whether you just graduated college or have been working for years, when you think about aligning your learned skills, your values, and passion with the question, *"How can what I want and what I know help others?"* you will start leaving a positive legacy, quite effortlessly.

For example, if you want to become a professional athlete, musician, or public figure, and you focus on yourself and how good you are compared to others all the time, you may pull back. Instead, you can realize that with your athletic or public status you will be a role model, inspiring others who watch in awe to be strong and courageous. You'll inspire others to think, "If they can do that, I can achieve what I want, too!" Eventually, you'll have enough people paying attention to you that you can use your voice and actions outside of your area of expertise to impact other issues you care about. Your legacy may become how fast you ran, how far you threw a ball, or how many Grammy-winning records you produced, but you will also be leaving a legacy connected to your kindness, attitude, mentorship of others, and what you took a stand for during your time in the limelight.

This can go for any field. I know coaching is powerful, and I take pride in helping those whose bottom line is not the money they earn but the meaning and the purpose of their work. They care more about the positive difference they make than the financial reward. That's not to say money is not flowing; it is, and that's often a reflection of the benefit they provide to others.

An entrepreneur will have a love for starting businesses, and there are infinite ways to do that. They can integrate thinking beyond themselves into the very foundation of a startup by considering the work culture being created, the benefits provided, the diversity in hiring, and the environmental sustainability of policies and procedures, to name a few things. As a founder, this is a time to connect to your values, think about your immediate circle of people and community, and the imprint you will be leaving as you go.

Each time we throw out our garbage, the bin it ends up in matters. Are we too lazy to sort one day? Out of convenience, are we buying greens in a tub of plastic that will have to be managed by hundreds of hands or left behind for generations? Those convenient choices are leaving a legacy.

Leaving a legacy can be as unique as you are. Someone who lives paycheck to paycheck today says: *I want to change my financial trajectory for my children and their future by learning how others who are more successful than I am think. I want to become unrecognizable compared to what was thought of my potential. This will impact the lives of my children and future generations.* And on the opposite spectrum, when someone inherits or amasses wealth and creates a foundation that, over the years, invests that money towards goals that make the world a better place for many, long after they have passed ... both of these individuals have a legacy and are leaving a huge gift.

There are so many ways to leave a positive impact. Perhaps you are a parent, a babysitter, or a nanny; remember that you are not only nurturing by managing basic care needs, but you are also bringing impressions of happiness and joy to another person and showing them that they are loveable. Perhaps you mentor youth, helping them to succeed. Perhaps you foster animals until they find a home. As an artist, you may be intentional about the images or works that you put out into the world. As a businessperson, you may be conscientious and work to become a B-Corp or a "Great Place to Work" company.

An act as simple as taking the spider that's in your home and placing it outside instead of killing it impacts the circle of life, shows your awareness, and quietly leaves a legacy.

Your legacy intention can take many forms. You may want to leave financial security for others. You may want to educate many. Perhaps you want to promote equity and justice for all or ensure that your creation or invention continues to be disseminated in the best way possible. Maybe you want to enrich the lives of others now, so their future is bright, and/or our global ecosystem is sustained.

Think of your life and work as a road map to this legacy. When you live a purpose-filled life you honor your core values, you trust yourself and your intentions, and you and others will get to reap the rewards of your impact in the near- and long-term future.

It's likely that projects you work on or people you help during your life feel immediate benefit and joy and, in turn, end up benefiting others long after you've completed your time here.

"If I am not for myself, who will be for me?
And being only for myself, what am 'I'?"

— Hillel

Money, People and Service

You can pray all you want, but you won't wake up one morning and find a huge pile of money in the middle of your living room floor unless you or another human put it there.

MONEY COMES THROUGH PEOPLE.

It's through your connections, relationships, and service to others that money comes. It passes from one person to another. If you're not in relationships, connecting, and giving of yourself, there's no path for money to come your way. As money flows to you and through you to others, you are consciously or unconsciously making an impact and leaving a legacy.

Think about how money has come to you and become aware of the human exchange factor. For example, you may have:

- Served people in a restaurant or café
- Coached, mentored, taught, or consulted
- Designed gardens, built furniture, made jewelry, or painted murals commissioned by others
- Opened a small business that served others
- Worked as a junior volunteer, nurse, doctor, or EMT helping those who were not well
- Worked to bring strategy and programmatic input to an NGO that served many clients

Unless you've inherited enough money to stop thinking about building wealth or you have won the lottery, I would venture to say that

TO IMPROVE YOUR WEALTH YOU NEED TO BUILD YOUR RELATIONSHIPS AND YOUR WILLINGNESS AND ABILITY TO BE OF SERVICE.

If you have an abundance of relationships and a service that's in demand, you'll also be flowing money to others who help you provide this service. When you choose to let go of certain tasks by hiring others to help you do them, you are allowing yourself to focus on your highest contributions. You serve more people in the way you do it best, while bringing work and professional development opportunities to others.

COACHING MOMENT

When you think of money and finances in terms of:

- The people and relationships in your life
- The services you're able and willing to provide
- The people who benefit and appreciate what they receive from you
- The way you approach staying comfortable or doing things outside of your comfort zone

What ideas come to mind that can shift things for you and take your abundance to the next level?

If finances are a struggle:

- How might you improve your ability to connect to others, so that more money can flow your way?
- How might you expand the amount of service you provide?
- How can you free up time for more by creating efficiency in your day by delegating tasks and streamlining your schedule and services?
- How can you leverage your relationships to bring more of your best services to others?
- How might you nurture yourself so you can be of service while remaining energized?

People don't typically walk around thinking about their legacy but maintaining some awareness of the topic throughout life can be a guide as you make life choices. I feel the biggest legacy we leave costs nothing, because

OUR BIGGEST LEGACY IS HOW WE TREAT OTHERS.

All the money in the world won't repair or make up for the mistreatment of others.

11

PASSION

Fire It Up!

I can't say enough about this driving force. When I talk about passion, I'm referring to an intense drive to do, change, or create something; a devotion to a person or cause; acting out of conviction; and for sure having two feet in with your heart and soul. When you're passionate, your willingness increases, and nothing gets in your way.

You can feel passion for an ideal, a goal, or people in your life. This passion drives you to BE more, DO more, CREATE more, and ultimately HAVE more of the results you're focused on. This passion will have you jumping out of bed in the morning, working into the wee hours, or spending a few hours on your project when you can't sleep. Your passion will drive you to dig deeper into your capacity, use every ounce of what you know, and tap into who you know to make what's in your mind's eye come to fruition.

It's not every day we feel intense passion and drive for something we're committing our time to, but when that fire heats up, I honestly have to say: if it is aligned with your values and life dreams, go for it. There's so much joy and adventure to be had in the commitment, chaos, and movement that will be created. You will learn more than you can imagine about yourself and others. You will move mountains and you will feel proud. It's in these moments or years of passion that we commit to people and projects and create legacies.

Writing this book was out of my comfort zone for a long time. I could find reasons all day long as to why it wasn't of value to pursue. Yet, the idea of writing a book kept nagging me. It was definitely on my back burner. Finally, I started to think that if nothing else, writing it would get the life and coaching framework I've adopted over the years on paper, and it would be there in a nutshell for my sons.

I have wavered many times, but I never lost the passion to write these thoughts down for my own children. Focusing on them and a few others, I relaxed about who I was writing for and was able to find my writing rhythm in a way that took pressure off the table for me. Then my vision of the book expanded to other young emerging leaders, and I started to feel comfortable with the idea that it could also provide reminders for my executive clients and others.

Ultimately, I held onto the vision of my sons reading it, since that was the stake in the ground for me. I used the question: *"Do I feel they need to know this?"* as a barometer of what to include and eliminate. By writing this book for my closest circle, I've been able to write it for you.

Think back to the times in your life when you were absolutely DRIVEN BY PASSION. Perhaps you left your job to do something bold, courageous, and meaningful to you. Perhaps you set your mind to a project and followed it through to the end. Maybe someone inspired you to connect to an organization you ended up caring deeply for. Recall how you felt and the value your passion-driven actions had on others and you.

COACHING MOMENT

Knowing that passion is a driver, what's on your back burner now that you truly care to make happen? It may very well be something no one knows or cares about, other than you. Plant your stake in the ground.

WHY does it matter to you?

What if you pursued your backburner idea?

- What three people would benefit? You can be one of them.
- What if you did it for just them and then let others benefit, if that is meant to be?
- What if you followed your heart just for you? Will you allow yourself that?
- What's the legacy (long-term benefit) that would result from you pursuing this passion?

Imagine living a life lit up by passion, with breaks to breath in between. Follow your passion to BE, DO, CREATE, and HAVE more and more of what lights you up.

Life Purpose

YOUR LIFE PURPOSE IS THE ESSENCE OF WHAT YOU BRING TO OTHERS WHEN YOU SHOW UP.

Your presence, your unique energy, who you are being, and what you do benefits others in a positive way. Your way.

Your life purpose isn't a convoluted marketing statement. It's what you bring in tiny increments with dedication, passion, commitment, and with a sense of loving duty. When you string all the tiny resulting acts together, they reflect your life purpose. As you relax and can see yourself without filters, your life purpose will become evident.

Think of the things you do that light your passion, honor your values, engage your devotion, and remember the times when you have been the most authentic and willing. Think of working moments when you actually feel like you're on vacation; you're doing activities that you would give freely if you didn't need money to thrive. What exactly are you doing? What is the through line in all those activities? The essence of what you're doing is your life purpose, which can be expressed and applied in many ways.

I've realized my life purpose is nurturing. It seems so simple, one word. That purpose can take many forms of expression, and each time I truly get to nurture, I feel joy, passion, and commitment. It has looked like me nurturing children, creativity, ideas, authenticity, courage, excellence, fearlessness, calm, and nurturing passion in others. It's also looked like nurturing myself and the many people in my life. I nurture friendships and give my nurturing to the organizations I care about. I get to see the results of my nurturing over time, receive deep satisfaction, and feel great gratitude for my life and purpose.

With your one word, you can come up with a life purpose statement. Knowing your own purpose will eliminate a lot of confusion about meaning, your motives, what you are drawn to, good at, and why.

When you think of one word or a short phrase to describe your life purpose, what comes quickly to mind?

COACHING MOMENT

How does your presence and energy benefit others? Do you bring calm, nurturing, and/or creativity? Do you expand vision and help others see greater possibility? Do you see the potential pitfalls and create security? Do you bring laughter to lighten a room? Do you exude courage, which inspires courage in others? Are you a teacher at the core? Perhaps you bring knowledge and facts to enlighten or make complex concepts simple to understand. What do you naturally bring to others when you show up?

Trust what comes to you and let that be your life purpose.

12

JOYOUS
ADULTHOOD

Creating from the Inside Out

Adulthood brings autonomy, freedom, and years to explore and play in the very garden that you plant, nurture, and sow. The more you are aware of what holds you back, work to heal the inevitable experiences and trauma that hurt you in your youth, and forgive and let go of what you no longer need to hold onto, the more powerfully you become immersed in your adult life and free to create and live your future visions.

At this point, you may realize that the very best that you are and bring to others emerged from your experiences, including the more painful ones.

The more you accept and welcome your adult authority, and realize you are the one creating and caring for your life and self, the more you will TRUST yourself, have SELF-COMPASSION, create STABILITY, and feel HOPE for your future. **When you love yourself deeply and nurture yourself completely (mentally, emotionally, spiritually, and physically), you will be living a joyous adulthood**. You will experience that the most nurturing and treasured love comes from within you first and foremost.

You'll know you're solidly planted in your Joyous Adult self when you're living life curious, flexible, inspired, creative, discerning, disciplined, capable, JOYOUS, and so much more. Look back to your notes from the exercise that established how you feel when expansive or constricted (pages 33–34). Those expansive feelings describe how you feel when your Joyous Adult is empowered.

Love, joy, authority, individuality, and freedom are amongst the most uplifting and expansive emotions you will feel. In your adult years, these emotions are internally derived from your own sense of agency and your ability to create well-being for yourself. A Joyous Adult has earned their own esteem and knows they will do what they say for themselves and others. All this will be reflected in the circumstances you create.

Your joy-filled emotions will stem from your gratitude towards yourself, your appreciation of who you are being in the world, the relationships you maintain, your well-being, and your ability to live fiercely, courageously, and passionately. How this looks will be very different in each person's unique life. These emotions can also stem from your connection with nature, the acts others do that touch your heart, and from appreciating the many ways humans are remarkable. And, if you have a relationship with the unseen, from the awareness that leaves you in awe. Expansive emotions stem from consciously and powerfully creating the life, impact, and connections you desire while being your most authentic self.

Joyous Responsibility

When you create circumstances that reflect your life visions and the desires you have for yourself and others, you will feel happiness and the sense of adventure on the journey.

TENDING TO THE DETAILS OF YOUR LIFE WILL BE A JOYOUS RESPONSIBILITY, AND THERE WILL BE NO SENSE OF BURDEN WHEN YOU TAKE ON CHALLENGES THAT ARE BIG, AUDACIOUS, AND ALIGNED WITH YOUR VALUES.

When you remain responsible for what is yours to care for, support others who want to be supported, yet don't lift more than you can manage, you will enjoy joyous adulthood. There is a clear distinction between Joyous Responsibility and burden. Understanding this will make a huge impact on your ability to live a joyous life.

COACHING MOMENT

Circumstances will deplete you when you are allowing boundaries to be crossed, taking on too much, being over responsive, or giving without replenishing yourself. This can land you on a slippery slope from Joyous Responsibility for your life and circumstances to feeling burdened.

Think of the people, things, and projects for which you feel Joyous Responsibility. These will be a natural reflection of and aligned with your core values being honored.

Now, notice if there are people, things, and projects which feel burdensome to you in some way. Feeling resentful, drained, overwhelmed, and angry will be clues to the burden you are taking on and carrying.

With awareness of the difference between Joyous Responsibility and burden, you can now choose what you want to keep, delegate, or completely let go of. All the while being diligent of what you take on moving forward.

Life is a playground, and your joyous responsibilities can be many.

Life as a Personal Development Opportunity

At times, your personal and work relationships, as well as life circumstances, will present challenges that reveal opportunities for personal and professional development. These trials and tribulations emerge, ideally encouraging deeper self-reflection and learning about ourselves. Similar to how children look for taller trees to climb or more adventurous amusement rides, for Joyous Adults, challenges serve as learning tools, empowering us to progress.

EMBRACE THE CHALLENGES AND LEARN ALL YOU CAN FROM THEM, WHILE STAYING ABOVE THEM.

You are not your challenges; ideally you are engaging and managing them to the degree that's appropriate for you to do so. You are also not your successes; you co-created them. You are your being, your nature and essence, and that remains constant regardless of changing circumstances or what you are doing or experiencing.

No matter whether you have a job, love your job, lose a job, or retire from your job, nothing has changed about the essence of your being. Your feelings may fluctuate, but your feelings are not you at the core. Over time, you'll want to connect to the you, the BEING that just is regardless of the rest.

Your successes, challenges, and circumstances are a reflection of what you are visioning and what you are choosing to do and not do; they are not you.

As much as circumstances can animate us, your adult self can celebrate successes, challenges, and even failures based on who you are being in the process of getting to your circumstantial outcomes. Who you are being reflects your imagination, your thinking, your perspective, your own stability, your emotions, and your capacity to process all of it. Your ability to ask for help, delegate, stay focused, and follow through has an impact. Who you are being has everything to do with your circumstantial outcomes/results. They are a reflection of you.

Be the Magician

You have beautiful dreams for yourself, your life, and the world. They will expand and deepen as you learn what it takes for you to realize your capacity to move something from vision to manifestation.

TRUST YOUR VISIONS AND DREAMS AND REMEMBER TO TRUST YOURSELF AND YOUR OPERATING INSTRUCTIONS.

Your devotion to your visions of the future and your willingness to dedicate yourself to those visions through the framework discussed in these pages, and other tools which you'll find along your own journey, will support you in the process of making your life one of dreams come true. Going back to the Wheel of Life, the space of time between where you are now and your vision holds your potential to create magic and activate everything needed to actualize your dreams. Committing to your future vision, you will learn to be supported and to provide support, to receive and to give, and to experience all the gifts of being alive. With time, your fears will give you cues and activate your inner guidance, as you courageously step into new territory knowing there's much to experience there. You will trust the process needed to create something from nothing, as you live life with two feet in.

MARIA CRISTINI is an executive coach and advisor to leaders and their teams. Her Daring Leaders Bold Ideas programs serve visionaries who lead philanthropic, non-profit, and positive impact organizations, businesses and projects. She is passionate about inspiring greatness in emerging leaders though her Ten Day Launchpad program. She has a propensity for seeing individuals and teams embrace their potential.

While on executive board teams and steering committees, Maria has led succession planning, organizational growth, fund development, merger acquisitions, inspired vision, and implemented strategy to support optimal outcomes. Maria's ability to create positive collaborations, her understanding of process and what it takes to get things done, is leveraged through her coaching, strategy and creativity.

Creating balance by making work and life fun comes easily to Maria. Daytrips and longer adventures with friends and family nurture and inspire her. mariacristini.com

DAWOOD MARION is a contemporary artist known for his superlative craftsmanship. He was born in Los Angeles and has been drawing since he could hold a pen. With a background in conceptual design and drawing mastery, he doesn't limit himself to any particular genre. Dawood has worked as a conceptual and character design illustrator in film and video games, illustrated books, created an instructional video series and executed two documentary films. He is consistently inspired by life, ideas, and testing his creative capacity. dawoodmarion.com

ALEKSANDRA JELIC is a multi-disciplinary creative based in Belgrade, Serbia. She graduated from Academy of Art University, San Francisco and has been working in graphic, web and identity design for 20 years. Aleksandra works with international brands and continues to collaborate, as a freelance designer, with numerous San Francisco Bay Area based companies and individuals. "Design is my passion."

Thank you for reading TWO FEET IN.

I'm excited to share downloadable worksheets and other exclusive gifts related to the contents of this book with you.

As a reader of TWO FEET IN, I invite you to engage with what I have to offer and check back often, as I'll be adding more complimentary resources throughout the year.

Visit: https://mariacristini.com/book/resources/

Please take a moment to write an online review. Your feedback matters to me and helps others find TWO FEET IN.

I appreciate you and look forward to connecting.

DARING LEADERS BOLD IDEAS DARING LEADERS
BOLD IDEAS DARING LEADERS BOLD IDEAS
DARING LEADERS BOLD IDEAS DARING LEADERS
BOLD IDEAS DARING LEADERS BOLD IDEAS
DARING LEADERS BOLD IDEAS DARING LEADERS BOLD IDEAS
DARING LEADERS BOLD IDEAS
DARING LEADERS BOLD IDEAS DARING LEADERS
BOLD IDEAS DARING LEADERS BOLD IDEAS
DARING LEADERS BOLD IDEAS DARING LEADERS
BOLD IDEAS DARING LEADERS BOLD IDEAS
DARING LEADERS BOLD IDEAS DARING LEADERS
BOLD IDEAS DARING LEADERS BOLD IDEAS
DARING LEADERS BOLD IDEAS DARING LEADERS
BOLD IDEAS DARING LEADERS BOLD IDEAS
DARING LEADERS BOLD IDEAS DARING LEADERS
BOLD IDEAS DARING LEADERS BOLD IDEAS
DARING LEADERS BOLD IDEAS DARING LEADERS BOLD IDEAS
DARING LEADERS BOLD IDEAS
DARING LEADERS BOLD IDEAS DARING LEADERS
BOLD IDEAS DARING LEADERS BOLD IDEAS
DARING LEADERS BOLD IDEAS DARING LEADERS
BOLD IDEAS DARING LEADERS BOLD IDEAS
DARING LEADERS BOLD IDEAS DARING LEADERS
BOLD IDEAS DARING LEADERS BOLD IDEAS

Made in the USA
Middletown, DE
14 December 2024